Rebellion of Quiet Things

A meditation on what it means to endure, reflect, and become

Authored by various global voices

Compiled by Quillkeepeers Press

Book Cover Design by Quillkeepers Press
Edit & Format by Stephanie Lamb

ISBN: 978-1-969601-06-4

Published by Quillkeepers Press, LLC
PO Box 10236
Casa Grande, AZ 85130

Essays, Flash Fiction, Memoirs, and Short Stories

Poems & Prose

Essays,

Flash Fiction,

Memoirs,

and Short Stories

Melanie White-Heron lives with an unreliable narrator in her head while still being a partner, a mother to three, one severely disabled and another with a mental illness) and a caregiver with the help of her Standard Poodle, Duke. She spent a career in love with teaching high school English and Media Studies, always as an amateur, continually learning, creating, and searching, until she collapsed into exhaustion each summer and retired. Her creative nonfiction has been published in *Thorn and Bloom* and in a McGraw-Hill textbook, and she excels at growing kale, ruminating on the past, and composting ideas from good books.

Seeking Comfort

The cup, her sweater, the wooden table, a soft click of her phone camera, and the image glows, effortless perfection in the heart-shaped milky froth, which will vanish with each sip. She decides to post it later. Around her, the cafe hums with routines like practiced dances where a close distance is maintained, where stepping near another risks injury, and where the performance of apparent connection matters. This particular location, a central part of the city, close to an enclave of established homes, buzzes all day, seating not guaranteed. He sees her, already seated, strides over while removing his coat, and notes her shoulders, pushed forward and lifted slightly in that demure, defensive way.

"Comfort. Some way of knowing what to expect. That's all. Nothing more. Just the feeling that everything's okay."

He had asked her what she wanted most in life, trying to surface the feistiness and passion he'd seen at work. He knew she'd respond, thought her answers might open a part of her, or at least give him a way in.

She pauses and breathes out through her mouth like a runner, spent before continuing. "Going to be okay. Might be okay and not fuckin..." She stops, looking up at him. "...chaotic."

He watches the way her face and hands move. Shifting her eyes to the green mug on the wooden table, her hands curl around it, right thumb through the small, round handle as if it were a fragile thing in need of care. Her full breasts, squeezed together by her arms, hover near the edge of the table, and he feels a warmth grow as he presses for more.

"And, right now, you're feeling like it's not. That everything's not okay?" The upward inflection makes it a question as he panics with this lapse in attention. Unease compels him to speak with effort, more cautiously than he does with other women. He thinks that might be a good thing.

She glares at him across the table, her brows squeezing the skin between them as he attempts clarification.

"I mean. I get you're feeling like it's not. But I was looking for more. Like an explanation, a description. To help me understand." He kept looking at her, noticing her unmoved expression. "More. Understand more." She felt his gaze like an intruder and shifted back an inch in the chair.

The espresso machine behind them wails as another shot of steam pushes out a thread of liquid into a small glass cup, then stops with a sigh of exhaustion. She reconsiders him and leans in. He follows, stopping with a few inches between their faces, his previous concerns slipping as she speaks.

"I can't remember when it changed. Maybe I learned it, picked it up from other people, or social media, I don't know, but there's always something...off. Something dangerous or threatening. Or about to collapse, just around the corner."

She sits back, waiting. He sits back until she speaks again.

"I feel this overwhelming sense of relief when I get home, and I see my mom's car in the driveway still in one piece." He watches her speaking, observing her long fingers and the way her lipstick is applied so perfectly. Red, his favourite.

"Or that our house hasn't burned down, or my dad hasn't." She leans in and lowers her voice, "Hasn't killed someone." Then looks over her shoulder, checking for witnesses before she turns back to him and says, "Or himself."

He swallows, now hearing her words, repeating them in his head, practicing what he had learned about paying attention. He lifts a blue ceramic mug to his lips, considering what to say, but she continues.

"Everything is so risky. It hasn't always been this way, but for our generation, it's risk after risk. If I decide to leave my government job for one in the private sector, I might be going from bad to worse. Everything feels so weighed down with expectations and outcomes. There are so many unintended consequences that we have to consider. Life is so random and chaotic. It feels like a single decision could destabilize everything." She pauses, sighing. "Nothing is reliable. Nothing is predictable."

This time, he doesn't think before he speaks. Instead, he does what he has learned, following the lead of his father, his older brother, and what he'd been learning about relationships, fulfilling the choreography of culture.

"Maybe you need a break. Turn off your notifications, delete your social media apps for a week, a month, and see if anything changes." He wasn't really seeing her now as his focus shifted internally. "There's these meditation apps. I've read a few articles about people who've done it, and they say it works wonders." He sits back in his chair and smiles.

And, there it is, she thinks – the Insta-answer. A deflating sensation, a collapsing of connection, a mutual understanding empties, filling the space inside her like toxic foam. A mild disgust rises in her belly. He clearly can not comprehend, does not understand her sensibility, or the tenuous nature of the world. She questions his intelligence, wonders if he has the ability to navigate the complex emotional terrain of the world, let alone the mind of a woman in her late twenties. A familiar pattern forms and repeats; she makes the decision there and then. No more intimate conversations with him. He can't handle it. And she can't stand the spontaneous combustion of disappointment.

After a pause, she tries to shift her face and says, "Yeah. Sure. I should give that a try." But, she can't hide the flat tone, the absence of energy, which comes with attempts to fake agreement. He sees through it, deciding to let her reply hang in the air without touching it. He notices the green of her turtleneck matches the colour of her cup, wonders if she chose it for that reason, then forces his focus back to the conversation. He hopes she might reconsider, thinks about making her uncomfortable with his silence. She should know what it feels like. His unease returns. Maybe this isn't a good thing after all.

She looks away from his gaze towards the door as if scoping out her escape route, tilts the green mug up to her mouth, draining the lees of her latte, twirling as she stands. They step outside into the afternoon sunshine, both suspended, hugging stiffly at shoulder height, mouthing the usual sounds that failed to mask a gnawing discordance, before they separate, moving in opposite directions down the traffic-filled main street, turn lights blinking, exhaust mixed with coffee and pastries.

His disturbance dissipates with each stride into the afternoon and vanishes as he steps into his shared townhome where he meets a barrage of questions from his roommates. He doesn't mind them asking about his dates or the teasing. Most of his male friends are still unmarried, though a few were in what he assumes are committed relationships. Now that he nears thirty, he thinks more about marriage and figures he isn't good at choosing women, this coffee date leaving him confused. He grabs the remote and changes the channel intending chaos. Shouting begins, followed by a few shoulder punches, swearing, and laughter, until it's snatched from his hands and the channel returns to the hockey game.

Her discomfort solidifies. She carries it on the walk home, holds it in her hands, and brings it up the steps through the front door of her parents' house. An urge to clean grips her, a familiar sensation. Despite remaining in her parents' home after graduation, she thinks of herself as entirely independent, perhaps anxiously confident. Still, she rationalizes that this decision supports her parents. She's good at cleaning, better than her mother, and takes the initiative to clean. Yet, their relationship has shifted only slightly from parent and child to roommates, with the same subtext.

She digs a black plastic pail out of the hall closet, grumbling at all the shit shoved into the small space, silently chastising her mother for not having a more organized home. At the sink, she waits for the hot water to run through, starts filling the bucket, and watches as the soapy foam steams. She lets out a growl, jumps at the shooting pain in her jaw and neck, forcing her to pause and stretch, remembering what her psychologist suggested. She leaves the partially filled bucket in the sink, which sloshes its disapproval at her ill-tempered movements, opens her mouth as far as she can, closes it, and starts swinging her arms back and forth while her body twists one way and then the other, imagining the magic spinner she made in grade three. Her eyes well, salty and stinging.

At the touch of her mother's hand on her shoulder, she jumps. She hadn't heard their arrival over the sound of running water, and this physical intrusion brings another snap of discomfort to her already quivering skin.

"What's wrong?"

"Nothing, Mom." She caught her mother's eyes, brows raised in doubt. "I'm fine."

From the hallway, her father pokes his head around the corner, smiles, then retreats, a move practiced and familiar.

"I saw you doing that thing. The arm swings."

"I know." She huffs. "It's complicated." She motions to the bucket, suggesting she's busy and not ready for conversation. Her mother's eyes shift to the floor while her body turns to the cupboards to shelve the groceries.

They had a history of short, terse disagreements, always unresolved, a pattern that developed in her teens and remained predictable. Conversations with her mother left her feeling mean and resentful. Her mother reached out, and she pushed her away, though this wasn't really what she wanted. Still, she couldn't help it, like well-worn grooves too deep to smooth.

Talking with her father was different. She saw him as struggling silently, managing the legacy of childhood abuse, though she didn't know the details. Something about time in foster care, or with an aunt, or some kind of displacement. When she did ask, he deflected with humour. They sometimes talked about politics, government policy, or making repairs to the house. But, he never asked about her life. He didn't ask about relationships or what she would do when they died, but she had thought about it. A choreography of conversation lived in her head, the subjects she could navigate with her father while her mother sat in the audience.

Staying at home during lockdown felt ethical, and at the time, it was easier than finding her own place amid all the disruption that came with it. But now that she was back in the office three days a week, her life felt less like her own, her loyalties divided, with too many people to consider, leaving her drained. Her days leaked, each one slowly releasing the air of passion and dedication like a helium balloon after a party. That inner drive she expected would carry her through a career of government service, nearly inaccessible. The pursuit of her degree had given her purpose; public policy work drove her impulse for change. But, now she felt less sure, more conflicted about her role in the way policies inadvertently exploited the natural world, the unintended consequences weighing on her. Conversations as attempts to reconcile her unease left her frustrated; the rigorous debates of her youth had evaporated. She thought she might be intellectually lonely, a term she'd once heard on a podcast.

She carries the black plastic pail into the kitchen and drops it on the floor, watching foamy suds spill over the edges. Dropping to her knees, she grabs a sponge from the bucket. She swings her arms around in circles pressing down on the floor, circling over and over, stretching her arms out in front. At the same time, her face hovers inches from the floor, scrubbing in circles over and over until her shoulder aches, and she continues repeating the pattern, muscle tension growing, spreading like tentacles along the right side of her body as she pictures an octopus suctioning its body around her.

Her mother turns from the cupboards and stands over her, watching for a few seconds before speaking. "You can't wash that away."

She stops scrubbing, the spell broken, and without looking up spits, "I'm not trying to wash it away. I'm just cleaning the fucking floor." Her temples pulse. "Seriously, Mum, you treat me like a child." Still on her hands and knees, she twists sideways to look up, discovering her mother's mouth wide, her face vacant, a second or two passing between them before her mother speaks.

"I meant that black mark on the tile floor. It's permanent marker."

Here it is again. That emptying and filling inside, that internal shape which marks so many of her conversations. Instead of anger, this time it's shame, then loss, like a sliding, no handholds, no grips. She kneels on the floor, exposed, naked, complicit.

She lifts her wet hands, sits back on her knees, her mother still standing with her shoulders curling forward in that familiar position which looks like the beginnings of a hug, her face working to translate, as if her daughter speaks a foreign language. On the floor, her straining body nudges the bucket, water sloshes, and foamy suds spill.

"Oh fuck," she whispers, watching the pool slide closer, knowing she has to live with the permanent black mark.

Jeffrey Beck is a retired Army soldier, essayist, poet, and a graduate student in the MFA program at Southern New Hampshire University. He earned his BA in English, summa cum laude, from American Military University. He lives with his wife on a five-acre homestead in southern Virginia, where he enjoys tending chickens, reading, and writing fiction, fantasy, and poetry. He is currently working on a memoir about his combat experience in Iraq. Jeffrey published *Letters to My Homestead*, his debut poetry collection, in September 2025 and has been published on poetry websites and in anthologies for Quillkeepers Press, *The Ariel Perspective* literary journal, *Poets' Choice* publishing, and *Perseverance & Resilience*, a veterans' poetry anthology presented by the Poetry Society of Virginia. Connect with Jeffrey on Instagram at j.b._leroy.writer.

Snowfall at the Edge of the Field

There is no announcement. The gray sky lowers, pressing its weight down and resting on the treetops. I can feel the air changing, and the crisp breeze brings the first flakes. Mother Nature confesses and exposes her secret: a nor'easter. The air presses pause, and she holds her breath; the snow begins to fall. Eventually, fences fade and vanish. The distinct outlines of the field and pasture blur into a single, solid bleached shape with no boundaries, leaving me to ponder the limitations we create for ourselves. The humming of everyday life halts, and the silence feels disorienting, like my place here is —or never was—my own. Yet nature seems unbothered by the changes. The birds and beasts of the forest take cover and rest, knowing there will eventually be a reprieve.

Inside the house, I feel protected. It is my shelter. There is warmth and candlelight, but no electricity, or murmuring appliances keeping a steady rhythm, just the silence of life on hold.

The snow forces time to loosen the grip of reality, making me revert to childlike memories. I remember the snow days of my past: the excitement of a day off from school, the packing snow crunching against the shovel, reinforcing the fortress walls from collapse, and hot chocolate to warm my frozen lips. The chicken noodle soup makes the house smell like comfort. The windows fog from the temperature juxtaposition, and I'd wipe a singular pane to see if the flakes were still falling, and I wished for another day home.

I don't realize until I slow down and observe, and the snow day forces me to measure the day by what I notice rather than what I produce. Sometimes it takes nature to tell us to ease the pace, to stay still; to make soup, to read, to steep a cup of tea, to dig out the watercolor paints. This stillness is unavoidable and never asks for permission. It is an inevitable and serendipitous gift—a reminder to slow down and be present. It is a hush and an adventure to rediscover small delights and spend time with yourself and with loved ones.

The next time the flakes begin to fall, look beyond the glass. Observe the boundaries and how they soften, how the lines between meadow and forest are erased for a short time. Watch how the quiet takes over. Rebel against the fast-paced world we've become and see how the land waits. Be patient with the white veil that coats your life, and wait with it.

Dempsey Strangeways lies in a desperate attempt to tell the truth. It comes out as speculative fiction, weird literary horror, and the occasional flash and micro oddities. A surrealist's eye for the macabre maps human minds fracturing under the weight of cosmic dread. They live in San Francisco.

Litany of Adoration to the Real Presence of Jesus in My Båhn Mì

I adore you, Lord Jesus, present here in my báhn mì as truly as in heaven. I kneel before you with all the love of my heart.

Holy Lord, I come before you in adoration. May your grace flow abundantly and heal all those who crave toasted baguette.

Christ Jesus, truly present in this blessed sandwich, you are the source of all grace and love. May I be as filled with your presence as you are with fresh cucumber slices.

Sweet Jesus, hidden under the appearance of pâté and fish sauce, You are the way and the life who has yielded this wholly awesome pork. Grant us a piece.

Blessed Lord, who was in the heart of that old Vietnamese lady who was up before dawn to bake this heavenly bread, grant us eats.

Blessed Christ, by whose cosmic design the rays of the sun shone down and nurtured the wheat, have mercy on us.

Sacred Host, thank you for going light on the cilantro.

Jesus, who taught us to pray in secret and not to erect massive crosses, have mercy on us.

Jesus, with us always until it's time to pay taxes, have mercy on us.

Jesus, who taught love thy neighbor, but probably never met my neighbors, have mercy on us.

Christ Jesus, who said we shall always have the poor and so now we do, we beseech You, hear us, O Lord.

For those who have not even this lemongrass or this mortadella to stave away hunger, hear our prayer.

That our exceptionalism does not mean rules for everyone except us, we beseech, O Lord, hear our prayer.

Lord, may we receive you frequently in holy communion with delicious condiments, hear our prayer.

God the Son, who witnesses 1 in 5 children going to sleep hungry in these United States, hear our prayer.

That we may forget any concept of "them" and recognize all of Your children as "us," we beseech You, O Lord, hear our prayer.

That we may some day see You face to face in the eyes of the least person among us, we beseech, O Lord, hear our prayer.

That we may refuse to suffer billionaires while Your sons and daughters have nothing to eat, we beseech you, O Lord, feed them.

Lamb of God, which I might try next time with pickled carrots, have mercy on us.

Amen.

Elizabeth Cohen, a former SUNY Professor of English and editor of *Saranac Review*, has an MFA in creative writing from Columbia University and edits a small press. Her work has recently been published in *Cagibi, Spotlong Review, Coachella Review, Reed Magazine,* and *Persimmon Tree.* She is the author of *The Hypothetical Girl*, short stories (Other Press), and *The Family on Beartown Road*, a memoir (Random House/Penguin). She lives in

Albuquerque, where she enjoys early mornings with rye toast and black coffee, followed by long walks with her somewhat feral dog, Layla.

Delivery Day

The Banned Books Club met on Thursdays, unless someone called for an emergency meeting, in which case it could be any day except Tuesdays, because that was the day Phoebe had no child care for Abraham. That would have been fine if he were a different kind of child, but he was the sort that was given to bouts of ear-splitting, inconsolable screaming. Nobody knew why he cried like that; it was as if he were being stabbed from within, to be honest, but just try to discuss a library removing "To Kill a Mockingbird" over the sound of that kid screeching. Although, as one member of the group remarked, "we should all be screaming, frankly."

Josie was late and hurried along West Tenth toward the small café on the corner of 7th Avenue to the meeting. The streets were empty except for various large, unmarked delivery trucks, unloading and loading up great boxes of who knows what. They double- and triple-parked on the narrow street, which caused a lot of honking from cars and Ubers seeking to squeak past.

The gutters gushed with red fluid that day, which Josie decided must have run down from the meatpacking district. Meat blood? Whatever it was, it was sloshy and unsettling. She stepped over it gingerly, trying not to let it overlap the tops of her boots.

Nobody ever went to Café de Montoya before noon, which was a damn shame, said Michael, the group's founder, because they made the best Torta Hispañola in town. Because he was concerned about the future of the teensy eatery and its proprietor, Montoya. It had been Michael's idea to have their meetings there. Once, when Josie asked the first name of this man with the tragic eatery, the answer had come swiftly: "Just Montoya." Montoya was a big man whose girth rivaled his height. He was supposed to be struggling, yet Josie couldn't help but notice he was always getting massive deliveries. If the café was doing so poorly, why was he always ordering so much food? Michael was the one who ordered everyone the "I read banned books" T-shirts. He had a lot of thoughts about banned books, but no answers to Josie's questions.

It was embarrassing to be running late, as today was the day the group would discuss the future of Josie's favorite book, *Bless Me, Ultima*. Not only was it being banned in various schools and libraries around the country, but word had it that it was publicly burned. This news came from a credible source and inspired Josie to call for an emergency meeting of the Banned Books Club on a Wednesday, which is very unusual. In fact, nobody could remember ever meeting on a Wednesday before. Banned book emergencies were rare.

By the time she arrived, the members were already assembled in the back, around two tables pushed together to make an eight-top. Three of them were sipping from Montoya's small porcelain mugs, coffee so dark and rich you could feel the grounds just waiting at the bottom of each cup to hit your tongue. The others had tall glasses of water. The smell of Torta Hispañola and frying potatoes lit the air with a rich aroma. "Hi, everyone," said Josie, taking the only chair left, which was across from Michael and Loretta, the other group organizer.

"Look whose gracing us with her presence," snarked Marjorie, the official group snarker, (in Josie's opinion).

"Damned #2 train wasn't running, I had to take the 1. Then it stopped for about five minutes at 23rd. Everyone was furious."

Montoya interrupted Josie's transportation soliloquy with a platter of freshly made Tortas, potatoes, and beans. The beans were so savory that they had once been written up in the Village Voice. The article, by one Betty Jones, was framed by the cash register, yellowed now and spotted with grease.

"Smells great, Montoya," said Michael. He thought of himself as the savior of the café, the same way everyone in the group felt they were potential saviors of banned books. Someone had to step up in this world. They were *that* sort of people, and they took great pride in meetings like this one, where they would talk about ways to "fight back" and "speak truth to power". But how exactly to save the banned books? This was the question the group got stuck on, time after time. They could write angry editorials. They could write praiseful essays about the importance of certain books. They could visit libraries and give impassioned speeches about the value of libraries in the canon. But they could not stop the enemies, the demonic book banners. And the book burners! Josie launched into the group meeting, talking about that. "This is 1933 redux!" she said.

"You mean 1934," said Michael, the group keeper of the facts. "In 1934, the American Library of Nazi Banned Books was founded in Brooklyn."

"Is it still there?" asked Marjorie. "Field trip, anyone?"

"I don't think so," said Thomas, who lived in and was therefore anointed as the group's Brooklyn expert. "It was in the Brooklyn Jewish Center on Eastern Parkway. Today it's some Hassidic place."

"So there is no banned books library, anywhere?" asked Marjorie, with a tone of horror.

"There kinda isn't," said Michael. "Of course, there are lotsa' traveling exhibits. And there is Banned Books Week, which we are commemorating with our exhibit at PS 1."

The group had been compiling books and getting quotes from various authors to prepare for the October 5th exhibit opening, just in time for Banned Books Week. This was something Phoebe had taken on as a project, maybe feeling bad because she often had to miss meetings.

"But no library, anywhere?" Asked Marjorie again.

"'Fraid not," Michael said again. To Josie's chagrin, the conversation had veered off from the burning of *Bless Me, Ultima*, Josie's favorite book by her favorite author, Rudolfo Anaya, which she had read in college and still remembered. The group had semi-stumbled on a nascent purpose that conflicted with her idea (which she had yet to present) of establishing a national "Ultima Day". It seemed like everyone was excited to start planning the relaunch of a banned-books library.

"I have to run to the bathroom," Josie said, annoyedly excusing herself. The back of the café was very busy, but not with the kind of back-of-café activity one might expect. In fact, there were no sous chefs chopping vegetables; no large pots overflowing with steamy, sumptuous, and fragrant contents. Rather, Josie saw a group of men moving around with determined focus, engaged in some kind of organized activity. For a moment, she imagined they might be unboxing banned books, as there was a secretive feeling in the kitchen, filled with large, unlabeled boxes. She immediately dismissed that thought as ridiculous. They were doing *something* with boxes; however, they were ripping them open frantically with box cutters. One man standing in the back was writing on a clipboard. As she turned the corner to the women's room, she glimpsed something she was clearly not supposed to see: a man, emerging from one of the boxes. He was a small, middle-aged man wearing what looked like pajamas. He looked very relieved to be getting out of the large box. The man who had cut open the box shook his hand, and then the small man, unfolding from the box, lurched into his arms. "Abrazo!" he exclaimed.

When she was seven years old, Josie had hidden inside a fold-out couch in another family's living room during a game of hide-and-seek with a group of children. Once she was folded inside, however, she quickly realized she couldn't figure out how to get out again. Meanwhile, the other children had forgotten their game and went outside to play in the backyard. But Josie remained folded on the couch, cramped and in mounting panic, her left leg growing numb from the position. "Help! Help," she cried out, but her voice was muffled; she wasn't sure anyone could even hear her. Is this the way she would die, folded in a couch, and unable to even get a good breath of air, she wondered?

Finally, one of the other children's mothers heard her and rushed over to open the couch. "You could die folded up in a couch like that!" the mother had said. She wanted to fall into the woman's arms; she was so relieved.

That phrase came rushing back to her now, when she saw the man getting out of the box. It was like the words had been waiting inside her mind all these years for an opportunity to re-emerge. But a box is not a couch, she reminded herself, just as she literally bumped into Montoya, who looked stunned to see her. Then, very unhappy.

"This," he said, "is going to be a problem."

"Oh, hi, Montoya," said Josie, as nonchalantly as she could muster. "I was just going to the ladies' room." As soon as she said it, she was struck by the antiquated sound of the phrase. Did anyone even say "ladies" anymore?

"Come with me," Montoya ordered, pulling her by the arm into a small alcove. Then: "What did you just see, Josie?"

"A lot of boxes," she answered.

"But what else?" he demanded.

"Montoya, are you yelling at me?"

"I'm sorry." The burly man quickly changed his tone. "It's a delivery day," he explained. "I'm tired."

"Okay," said Josie, "I get it. But may I have my arm back now?"

"Of course," said Montoya, immediately letting go of her arm. "But when you are done in the bathroom, please go out the back door and then back in through the front. We are busy back here, and make sure everyone knows!"

"Okay, okay," Josie said. She went out the back and then back in through the front door, and just as she did, she ran into Phoebe, who was carrying

Abraham. They went in together and sat down. The group discussion was still focused on reclaiming or relaunching the museum of banned books. Clearly, the group had moved on from the burning of her favorite book, the purpose of the emergency session, she reminded herself.

"Anyone need anything else here?" Asked Montoya, who had walked to the back corner of the café, where the group was assembled. "I'll have a milkshake," said Phoebe.

"What about you, Josie?" Montoya asked, looking her right in the eyes. "Do you need anything else today?"

"I'm fine," she said. Just as she spoke, baby Abraham started to wail. Phoebe took him outside to calm him on the street, walking back and forth.

"I'll see if I can help out," Josie said, brushing by Michael and Loretta to get to the door. By the time they came back in again, the group was getting ready to depart. Montoya made the milkshake Phoebe ordered "to go" in a big cup. He said farewell to everyone at the door, with its little bell that would ring every time someone opened it.

Josie was the third to leave and headed back toward the #1 train. She'd been too rattled by what she had seen and also by Abraham's cries (why did Phoebe bring him anyway?) to try to bring up *Bless Me, Ultima* again with the group. She realized she'd changed her mind somehow. She barely cared about it being banned or even burned. The author was dead. People already owned it or could order it from Amazon. Babies, she reminded herself, cry.

Just as she stepped off the curb at Fourteenth Street, a large box truck came careening around the corner and sent her flying, up, up into the air. People walking and even driving stopped to stare.

For a moment, when she was airborne, Josie looked up and saw the shape of an old bank that was now a nightclub called The Bank. Note to self: go to the Bank some night, she thought. Then she saw the sky opening up, beyond The Bank above her, bluer than she had ever noticed before, dressed in the smallest, crooked clouds. Some small birds sitting up there (were they sparrows? She thought they might be) took off at once, then vanished.

What are the last thoughts you will ever have in your life? Will you think about all the people you have loved? Will you remember a song, poem, or book you have loved? Josie hoped the people in the boxes would be okay. Maybe, she thought, Montoya would make them Torta Hispañola, with those crunchy fried potatoes and his famous beans.

Nathan T. Ashworth, a stroke survivor, is always looking for more: more from himself, more from literature, and more from life. At 40, he rededicated himself to writing and is currently opening up his life for the world to see. He writes to help people reclaim themselves through acceptance and meaning and focuses on providing a new take on personal identity and the ability to live life more consciously. Hidden then, living now. He writes on Substack at A Man Incomplete.

In Solitude, My Mistakes Make Me Grin

When I was eighteen years old, just released from the hospital following my stroke, I was offered the chance to speak, live and in person, to what I believed was a small group of people about what I had been through. I was having remarkable success with rehab, was planning on going back to school in the fall, and I was thinking about all the positive things that I would say. I am an optimist at heart, and I believed that I would "wow" the small assemblage of people with my story and my encouragement.

So...I didn't practice. I didn't write out my words. Who cared, right? I thought I would simply wing it, and the small cluster of people who came to the hospital would marvel at the fact that I had battled through this and thrived. I believed I was on the fast track to stardom post-stroke, in my own little way.

However, when I went into the conference room in the hospital and witnessed what was about to transpire, my heart shriveled up, and I immediately shut down. Three or four TV stations were there, with bright lights shining down upon me and news personnel all around. Forty to fifty people were in attendance, not the five to six I thought I would be speaking to. The PR director, whom I didn't even know what "PR" meant at that time, was there to greet me and shake my hand, hurrying me up onto the stage. All within thirty seconds of my arrival.

To say that I was shellshocked would be an understatement.

Obviously, I floundered. I believe I said one or two sentences about the tingling sensation that I experienced right before my stroke, but I couldn't think of much else to say. I didn't come prepared and didn't put the three or four things I was planning to say into bullet points. I didn't look up at the crowd and declare some sort of mind-bending thought or thoughts. I was lost and clueless for the twenty or so seconds I was "on stage." As I was returning to my seat, the PR director said something to the effect of: "...ok, well...thank you, Nathan, for sharing!" as she quickly rose and thanked the members of the press and the public for coming to the event.

I will remember that day for the rest of my life, not only for the fact that I couldn't think of the correct words to say (or any words to say for that matter!), but also for the fact that I failed to inform the large group what I had been through and how my stroke had affected my life. I know now that I should have gone ahead and practiced my speech, should have written more than two blurted-out sentences, and should have done a much better job at preparing myself for the unknown.

It has been twenty years since that fiasco happened, and I chuckle every time I think of it. I smile at being so incredibly oblivious. Yes, the entire event could have gone better. I could have shined. But as a highly introverted youngster who didn't have any idea what the rest of my life was going to look like, I think I did pretty well, all things considered.

****

Self-acceptance is far easier when no one is around.

When no one is looking at you.

When no one is judging you, laughing at you, or criticizing you. When there aren't forty or fifty people in the audience and TV stations itching for a scoop or an angle.

Now, when no one is around, I can laugh at myself. I will sing in the shower, be a horrible dancer (because I am), and acknowledge that in my own small world, I have many faults. When I am with my family, I can joke in my dry, easy-going way. When my wife and I are alone, we can literally scream with laughter.

But when I am around others, particularly around others at work or in an area where I don't know the "rules," I sometimes commit errors that

I am embarrassed about. Angry about. Sometimes they are more egregious, sometimes they are minor. But every time I make a silly mistake around people I don't know, I blame myself.

I blame myself with abandon. Unfortunately, there are times when I shut down and give up. There are times when I give away my agency and totally remove myself from the situation. I know that shutting down and relinquishing my influence never works in the end, but I do it anyway. I revert to my past and give up the power that I have. Whether it's therapy or my own reflections, I acknowledge that part of myself and work to continuously correct it. If I am in a small crowd, my mistake doesn't seem as big. But, the bigger the crowd, the more I feel pain if I make even the smallest of stumbles.

In solitude, I can easily shake the frustrations out and be on my way. I can, and do, modify my relationships to the outside world and become a better person. But when I try to do this in the company of others, I nosedive. Hard.

In *On the Brink of Everything*, Parker J. Palmer speaks of the Taoist master Chuang Tzu's telling of a man who is crossing a river in a small boat, only to realize that another skiff, without a boatman, will crash into his boat. After the crash happens, the man does not become angry, as most people would, and the lesson that Tzu is conveying is this:

Empty your own boat as you cross the river of the world.

In solitude, as my story could easily tell you, I can empty my own boat. I can make mistakes over and over again. I can laugh and not give a hoot.

But when I am with others, concerned with my own insufficiencies, I am absent with myself. And when I am absent with myself, I am not being fully present —not to myself, and not with others.

Going forward, I know that I will need to get over this hump if I am going to be a whole person, a person with a polyhedral sense of myself and what I represent to the world. If I choose to be that whole person, I will inevitably be a *better* person.

Solitude, I believe, is one way to overcome that fear that everyone has within themselves: of blame. Of the unknown. Of finding fault. Solitude is not loneliness, nor is it isolation. It's the state of being alone, but by being alone, one has the opportunity for growth and expansion.

Solitude is about being present with ourselves, whether or not we are with others.

Tadeo Ward is an aspiring writer and endurance enthusiast who lives in Lima, Peru. He graduated from Williams College with a B.A. in Comparative Religions, and is currently an MFA candidate with VCFA.

Sweat Talk

It was late afternoon on an average sort of summer day. Even before we hit the small knoll in Plainfield, I could tell something was off. It's hard to hide on a tandem. Today, she was unusually quiet. Equally telling, there was a slight lag in her upstroke and a reluctance to catch the higher cadences I offered. By the time we attacked the knoll, I had resolved to ask what's going on, but I waited until we cleared the short hill on the other side of town. Past that climb, we had a few miles of gentle rollers.

After breathing stabilized and as I tightened the gears, I called back, "What're you thinking about back there?"

There was usually a pause. I didn't mind waiting. My eyes were on the road. Green hills rose above, and fields sparkled in the river valley on either side of us.

"I am worried about Ariel."

Our children were a frequent topic during *'HAHA'* time. Ariel, our oldest daughter, was entering the early phases of adolescence and confronting the related risks and pressures. The influence of one friend in particular worried us. While Daysi and I found common ground in the fears we shared, our instincts about how to help ran in opposite directions. My wife usually wanted to clamp down, while I was inclined to step back and open up. The more worried we were, the more tightly we held onto our preferences.

She talked through a recent incident. I asked some questions. We were already accustomed to the deep privacy of our rides. All that we needed was that specific glance at the dinner table for a subject to be taken out of circulation and hung beside the helmets and gloves. By the time I broached the subject, we were a mere 25 minutes into a 2-hour ride. There was nothing but sweat and heavy breathing on the agenda for the next 90 minutes. Ariel was not standing behind us waiting for an answer about a sleepover. Her little sister wasn't lingering in the doorway. I didn't need to *get my point across* so that I could get back to a business call or out to the garden, or, or, or –– I wasn't going anywhere that took me more than 24 inches from my wife.

This day, I asked a couple of more questions. In part, I was stalling. We were about to turn onto the biggest climb of the ride. By habit, we stopped at the flower garden just after the turn but before the hill. The stop itself required a change in topic. I spoke up to confirm that we would be stopping and that I would loosen up the gears. The garden had a variety of lilies that weren't doing well at our place, and they were mixed with columbines in a combination we had never considered. The next 40 minutes were completely consumed in the exertion of the climb, and for 15 minutes after that, only whistling wind filled our ears.

By the time we hit the next section of flats, all of my "Yeah, but..." responses had burned away. I had spent the last hour sitting with the fears I hold. They had been ground through 3 miles of dirt road climbing, dragged alongside the pristine pond where we catch a quick break, brought over the unimpressive crest of the ridge, and buried beneath the hunt for potholes and rocks that is part of any descent. In every instant of that hour, my wife is present. I feel her in my quads. I hear the labor of her breathing. Of course, we talk across this hour, but it is in the clipped transactions of effort and beauty. "Rough spot, up here." I huff. "Look at the heron," she said. "Water lilies are going by", I noted. "Lots of cars at the store today," she observed.

Maybe enough had been said about our daughter's situation for this day. Perhaps it was enough for Daysi to share what she had seen and explain what it meant to her. There was no lag in her cadence. Her silences now felt more a part of the ride instead of apart from it. Let this thing be. My fear was a shade of darkness that has a hard time resisting the heat, salt, and fluffy clouds of a summer afternoon. Like so much of what was going on in our lives, the bigger issue ran deeper than any one event. With a bit of reflection, it was harder to see the urgency and easier to see the deeper pattern of our daughter's growth.

I chose to speak. Of course, I had some lingering suggestions about what we should do, but those mattered less than the emotion behind them. My deeper anxiety was that the world would try to break my child before she was equipped to defend herself, and the realization that this was already happening in ways that I couldn't even see, much less understand. I was pinned in the hope that she would figure out how to carve her path through it all, and the absolute certainty that neither Daysi nor I could save her from this struggle. The best we could do was to offer help, and the best help we could come up with was some mix of guardrails and the open road.

We had two more significant hills still on the ride, and one delicious paved descent where we tucked into all the velocity gravity could give us. In each, we gave our voices over to the ride —-oxygen relinquished to lungs and legs. We fought: gravity, pain, doubt. If only for this instant, in this tiny, arbitrary, and self-inflicted trial we triumphed — together.

We ended the ride with no clearer action plan than we had started. *'HAHA'* time had a funny way of eroding action plans, and yet the best options were always a bit clearer. Understanding was written across the landscape. We had just spent two hours in sync. Foot to foot. Thigh to thigh. We both said our piece. The details would work themselves out later.

Rajeshwar Prasad, born in Bela, Aurangabad, Bihar, India on 26 August 1970, is a poet, playwright, novelist, essayist, researcher, philosopher, thinker and academician. He is a prominent figure in English literature who infuses meaningful philosophical insights into appealing stories. With a Ph.D. exploring Christopher Marlowe's lyricism and many years of service as a Professor, he draws on the strengths of both worlds. He is the author of many thought-provoking plays, including *The Travellers, The Wife, The Tribute, Zero into Four, Teachers Day, Zero into Nine* and *Zero into Plus*; the insightful fiction, *Righteousness*; and collections of powerful poetry, including *Gandhi – the Messiah and Bullet Land*, all published by TSL Publications, Rickmansworth, UK. His epic, *The Gandhi-Gita*, the novels, *Dance of Democracy*, *Now, Forever Yours,* and the reflective essays in *Hello Life* show the author's scope. His life of teaching and creative writing demonstrates his commitment to enhancing mind and soul. He has been honoured with several national and international awards in Literature and Education. He has also published 26 research articles, 13 essays, short stories, and poems. His philosophical, humane, and thought-provoking articles were featured in *The Aerial Perspective*, Quillkeepers Press, LLC, US, and his articles were greatly admired and read. He was awarded the

Asian Excellence Award 2024 for the Best Professor of the Year, the Award of Excellence for the Indian Icon Educational Entrepreneur, 2 Times Golden Book Awards for his books Zero Into Four and Dance of Democracy, 2 Times Sahitya Sparsh Awards for his books *The Travellers* and *Gandhi – the Messiah* Top 10 Rising Leaders Awards, Top 100 Leaders Awards and Ukiyoto Literary Awards for his fiction *Righteousness*, Visionary Indians Award 2025, and National Teacher of the Year Awards 2025. For him, teaching and writing are not merely professions but sustenance for the soul – endeavours that allow him to continuously engage with and contribute to the literary and philosophical discourse.

The Unspoken Bloom

On the deliciously fertile banks of the slow-moving Adari River, the secluded village of Bela exhibited a study of profound, humbling contrasts. Raj was the product of this backdrop – a family where shortage was the norm of life but where morality, mutual regard, and sacrament, although invisible, flowed beyond limits. His mother and father, Bhagw and Jagad, took the earth's powerful wisdom through their calloused hands, their spirits uneducated but bursting with survival stories.

Raj was the eleventh issue among twelve tries at life. A harsh balance that resulted in eight siblings dying of the period's brutal, invisible killers: cholera, smallpox, and typhoid. The extremely high child mortality rates, deeply rooted in areas without basic health facilities and education, made surviving a statistical exception. Raj was a divine child, the last man standing who bore the heritage of the dead ones; thus, he was the silent centre point of his family's love. He was the most passionately loved, the last, and the exponent of all their unvoiced wishes.

Nevertheless, this dear eleventh son was a fragile story. From his birth to his eighth year, a lingering, slow-acting typhoid had affected him, making him very thin, a shadow among the healthy children of Bela. His troubled health was not considered a problem but a feature of common, universal affection; the whole community loved the weakest among them as a group, sharing a protective sigh and the recognition of life's delicate hold.

However, his family, which was fully dependent on the backbreaking work in agriculture and animal husbandry, needed everyone, no matter their lack of education. But, in those days, a necessary, people-centred movement was rooted. Education in Bela was merely a minor form of resistance to the status quo. Most of the time, the government's promise of learning would be a passing classroom shelter under the big, silent Siris tree or a temporary crowd in the village temple during heavy rains.

It was in these modest, changing havens that the outstanding teachers – Suresh, Ramchandra, and Sushila – were waging a silent fight to ban ignorance. They accepted that real work extended beyond writing on the board and teaching. They were not just waiting for the students; their mission was to uplift the country's very foundation, so they were hunting for places where the seeds of future pupils could be found, going through the villages patiently, meeting people face to face, and teaching with deep, steady grace.

Raj, who was very conscious of his duties on the farm and who was naturally weak, first made his own small, quiet opposition. When the teachers came, he was hiding among the thick stalks of the bean crops. He was softly taken, not forcefully dragged, to the knowledge he instinctively dreaded. However, that first day was a shock even to him; it was a revelation against all his physical limitations. The body that was weak could not hold back the mind; it reached out for the teachers' congratulations, and the teachers were speechless. The first fear disappeared and was replaced with the deep, resonant satisfaction of understanding. He became a student of fierce, silent sincerity.

His teachers, realising that there was great talent in the weak body, did their best to protect him. While the stronger students were given the tougher cleaning and hauling gradually, Raj was left free to engage in the intellectual work, which made him excel in every competition, turning his disadvantage of a physical nature into one of intellectual supremacy.

As he improved and passed his matriculation examination, the people of Bela set out to apply their usual norms, which meant a cultural background of early marriage; a habit that tied the ambit of the person to that of the family. Many marriage proposals came from the son of the family, who was loved and was very bright. His parents, who were steeped in tradition, were inclined towards saying yes. But Raj, who had mastered the language of delay and the power of the silent command, performed his most significant act of rebellion. Without any demonstration, he stated his disobedience to everyone, steadfast and clear. He will not get married before he accomplishes his ambition: to get a Post-Graduate degree, to be employed in the civil service, and to make his dream of being an English teacher come true. This was the quiet revolt – an unalterable pledge of a fate much greater than that which was determined by the rich soil of his birthplace.

The lustrous world of academia, with its tantalising promise of intellectual delight, was most loyal to Raj, its youngest and brightest disciple. His hallmark was Professor Rambilas, a perceptive, wise, and a man with deep understanding, who in him saw a rare genius at work. The Professor was not just transferring knowledge; he was cultivating visions, foreseeing Raj not only as a student but also as a teacher of

English, shining in the realm of knowledge. This conviction, a soft echo of fate, inflamed in Raj the thorns of fierce dedication and honesty that he treated not as a burden but as a celebration of his commitment. He handled his academic career with such understated elegance that he was always the top scorer in his classes, and eventually, his Master of Arts in English resonated with his academic brilliance all over the college.

However, the road to a professorship was not a short, easy one, with academic success celebrations along the way. He had to face the unavoidable Doctor of Philosophy or the National Eligibility Test as hurdles on his way to his dreams. It is also at this point that the subtle, sneaky biases of society began to work against him. No matter how smart he was, several professors quietly and firmly refused his applications for research projects. The silent reality was a heartless reflection of societal prejudices with deep roots: Raj belonged to the "weaker section," a label that was often more powerful than skill in the realm of higher education. Most professors from the so-called "upper echelons" were inadvertently the guardians of an exclusionary system.

Raj was still overcoming these silent barriers in his academic journey when another, not less potent, rebellion was simmering in his residence. His ambition and quest for knowledge were considered an attack on the established pattern of village life. His deeds were not "in line with the village culture," a stringent system that considered his academic seclusion an antisocial deed. His relatives, not knowing the burning fire inside him, that he should marry, kept pressuring him non-stop. If he didn't, they threatened with a boycott—a terrifying kind of social exclusion. For over 13 years, Raj had politely but firmly turned down several dozen marriage proposals, and with every rejection, there were more voices of disapproval and a growing bad reputation of his parents' shadowing them.

Then it was the day of a watershed moment, a confrontation between the past and the dawn of a new era. Raj, with plans to master two fields simultaneously, chose to pursue a second Master's degree, this time in Journalism and Mass Communication. As he was on the way to Magadh University, carrying not only books but also his dreams, he met his elder brother, Das, at the temple of the village. They conversed for only a few moments, and it was brutal in its finality.

"Where are you going with a bag and baggage?" Das demanded.

Raj, as a scholar who is sharing his vision, explained his aim.

Das, instead of supporting it, answered with a blow that knocked the wind out of him: "Reading will not be your life; hence, you should keep the bags at home and work with us only."

The words didn't disappear right away from the spot where they were thrown, as they were loaded with the expectations of several generations. Stunned into silence, Raj, with the unspoken order wafting louder than any shout, turned back. His bags, which symbolised his dream, were now just a burden, but in that moment of withdrawal, a quiet determination started to be formed. He still hadn't given up on English, for which he was still waiting for results; he would frame a different plan to make it through – his silent revolt against the imposed silence.

The village, seeing his status as an unmarried man, was talking in low and almost whispering, critical voices.

They said, "Raj is unsociable. The family and heraldry are not getting a good reputation from him. This is not the culture of our village. He is an immoral person who doesn't listen to the family members."

Besides this tireless social inspection, Raj's contemporaries were not only wedded but also nurturing their families, which further aggravated the moral pressure borne not only by Raj but also by his parents and the family, who grew irritable. The moment when his father, Jagad, out of patience, went too far and issued an ultimatum is the climax of this frustration.

"You must be married or else," Jagad said fiercely.

He continued, "I will marry Shiv, who is my grandson, and at his marriageable age. You have caused the family honour to be ill-famed. I won't wait for you. I don't want to see you, unmarried, under any circumstances. This is the last warning to you."

Raj, who was remarkably calm as the storm raged around him, replied with great confidence. "I surely do realise all the things around, but still, I will bring to your honourance my own self, also your entire family will secure the maximum honour because of me in the future, not today, but highlighted one day due to my good works, so please do not be anxious and just allow me a year only. I will get success for sure."

However, Jagad, whose view was dominated by societal expectations and the shame of the family, did not accept it. In fact, he had already moved on to secretly inviting relatives, getting ready for the marriage of his grandson, a public announcement of Raj's failure to fall in line.

The advice of former suitors, "One day even a dog will not ask you to marry, and you will be unmarried your entire life," was now coming back to haunt Raj with increased intensity.

Thirteen years of being mocked and threatened had eroded his spirit a lot, but the ultimatum from Jagad was beyond his limit. It was more than a threat; it was quite a betrayal from his father, a cut of the deepest of bonds among the family. Raj felt very devastated, and his body was also becoming weaker from the hardship. Nevertheless, strangely enough, his spirit, like a spring compressed by a great force, kept growing. It was like he was re-enacting Newton's third law of motion, with each external force making the internal force greater. So he simply bore down with more consciousness and determination towards his studies. A very alienating, painfully situational dynamic in which he's experienced total loss of companionship and family support, leaving him only the light of guidance from a distance, but still present with Professor Rambilas.

But Raj was not the type of person to look back and lose courage. He was quietly but fiercely devoted to his goal. He knew that there was unspoken envy and secretive designs from his family. As a result, he started to put in more work, but he was even more silent than before. His actions were hidden, and so were his hardships. None of those around him talked to him or offered him financial help. He was on his own, and he managed his money in ways that were not very clear.

The esteemed guru, Professor Rambilas, was the guiding light that Raj depended on so much. The Professor's generosity went beyond money; it was an investment in human potential, a philosophical gamble.

"Mr. Raj," he had assured, with his voice conveying the strong conviction.

He continued, "I shall support you financially until the moment you take my place as a professor. The repayment of the aid is only made when the recipient is successful; if the opposite happens, it should be treated as a non-refundable debt paid with my belief in your goodness."

This assurance became the silent anchor against the upcoming troubles.

Motivated by this profound trust, Raj plunged into his work. Within two years, he managed to secure his PhD registration under the strict supervision of Professor Somnath, who was as gentle and scholarly as Professor Rambilas. The following years were ones of trials and tribulations that finally led to the cherished degree. In fact, he was just the second person in his small, traditional village, after Shivkumar, to get so far – a deep but quiet victory. At the same time, he had passed the National Eligibility Test, which qualified him to pursue further professional studies.

His plan to obtain a government professorship began, with great care, under the tutelage of his academic mentor. He kept it secret, and that was like his delicate revenge against people's expectations.

On the other hand, the closer he got to his professional dream, the less warm the home atmosphere was. Instead of being a haven, his family turned into an area where he was being silently harassed. The death of his mother, a few years ago, due to a very sudden and severe heart attack, was a loss that broke his heart and took away his only emotional support. Now he was being refused the bare minimum that would sustain him – not only financial help but also the simple and humane nourishment of whey, curd, or milk.

This was not only neglect; it was a carefully planned hatred, a moral cancellation embodied in the act of denying sustenance.

He was absolutely alone, with no family, friends, or any other kind of support to help him. However, he still showed up and let his thoughts consume him in a great fight between heartfelt pain and a strong resolve.

"I am not denying that I am walking the true path of virtue," he said.

He used to say when no one was around, "It is the first step for the future of my family and society as a whole. My unshaken belief is my only co-traveller, even though I am going solo. I will get the success that I desire not by loud talking but by continuous low profile."

Raj learned to restrain himself from reacting negatively. His non-speaking role became his most effective form of resistance. Although relatives refused to communicate with him, he nonetheless acted as if the modus operandi of the house was the same as the one under which the disputes had been handled. The huge exertion of energy he made, the very strong will to succeed very fast, was totally hidden from all those who were around. Nobody could understand the burden of his resolve until the day the unexpected happened.

He had submitted his application and went for the interview for the post of Assistant Professor in Prayagraj.

Then, the miracle: A deep, silent revolt discovered its voice. Despite the wrongs and deals made against him, the interview's outcome was announced. Raj was among the people determined for the post. It was reported that he had been selected as an Assistant Professor of English.

The shock was of a great magnitude. This success was against all odds for Raj, his family, and the dozens of villages that were around it. The sceptics became supporters at once, their doubts turning into praises of his integrity and determination. The story went viral: the unintelligent boy of the past had become Professor Raj.

In a vivid manifestation of social expediency, the world recalibrated its centre. The proposals for his marriage that were once only from peasant families were now not only from peasant families but also from highly prestigious people such as judges, doctors, officers, and professors. His suffering was not recognised, but his success was rather remarked and celebrated. This instant and overpowering recognition was the chief moral paradox: the planet staging its ultimate acceptance of the prize while purposely neglecting the cost paid in silence and lonely virtue.

Raj did not dominate with a loud voice; rather, he went through life with the steady, calm current, which was different from the traditional way of doing things. While others saw only shortcomings, he saw opportunities, showing that he was slightly rebelling against the world by living by his own principles. But, even when public praise finally decided to focus on him, he still remained sad in silence, and a memory of his past success still haunted him. His academic mentor, a lone support, was the only one who knew the deep, unspoken grief that caused tears despite success.

His family, who had once been puzzled by his unorthodox dignity, now enjoyed his reflected fame.

His father, Jagad, with words full of late pride, said, "Son, you have decorated our lineage! Your different walk, with its quiet virtues, was something we were blind to. Let's now find you a partner who is intellectually worthy of you. Raj, well done!"

The affection of acceptance was like a new, unrealised expectation in the gesture.

Alexander Jones has an English/Creative Writing BA. After graduating, he went to trade school for metal fabrication. He's placed short stories or poetry in Akashic Books, *Bastion Magazine, Crack the Spine, DASH, Eunoia Review,* and other publications. One of his essays won GoRail's 2012 contest, while others have been anthologized by 2Leaf Press. He's slowly earning a Master's Degree in Holocaust and Genocide Studies. He works as a welder for a metropolitan transportation agency near New York, and lives with his wife and son in New Jersey.

The New Normal

I grab the flaking wrought iron railing with my right hand, plant my good leg, my right leg, squarely on the first cement step in front of me, and pull myself up. Then I swing my bad leg up, and pain flares from a constant dull ache to a sharp crescendo as I place my bad leg beside my good one, but the pain isn't too bad, and that's part of The New Normal. Last, I slip one of my crutches into my left armpit and use it to redistribute my weight.

Step one—done.

Eleven more to the front door of my apartment building.

Without letting go, I slide my right hand up the railing about a foot. Looped around my right forearm is a plastic bag from the drugstore with my painkillers inside. I've also got fresh bagels, and the moist, garlic-saturated warmth wafts past my chin.

I'm going to get up the other eleven steps, get inside, and take my painkillers first thing, while I'm still standing, before I park myself on the couch and eat my bagels.

Unless I dissociate, obliviate, float away on a sea of cognitive dissonance, passing in and out of sleep without being aware of it, like hearing a noise and turning my head to investigate and then, sometime later, wondering 'Why is my head turned? Why have I been staring at the corner of the room like there's something there, but there isn't, when I'm really just trying to watch TV?' In which case, I'll eat my bagels when I return to consciousness later, even if they're a little stale by then.

Juggling my weight between my grasping right hand, the crutches in my left and my bad leg, I step and plant the good leg again and pull myself up again. Then swing the bad leg up behind me again and stabilize with the crutches again.

Step two.

The New Normal has made my good leg much stronger; my calf is now a dense, tense, tight horseshoe from hopping and hobbling around. Having a 'bad leg' and a 'good leg' is also part of The New Normal.

Step three.

I'm now a quarter of the way up, and I've broken a sweat, and I need to fiddle with the plastic bag around my right arm, so I stop for a moment. Catch my breath. Roll my neck until there's a satisfying pop.

After standing here for a little longer than I need but not as long as I'd like, adjusting the stray loop of the plastic shopping bag, I slide my right arm up the railing and lurch back into action, carefully stepping with the good leg. Pain arcs up and then subsides as I put my weight on the crutch under my left arm.

Step four.

The loop on the plastic bag rides up again, and there are rusty paint flecks on its outside. Is it lead paint? Are my bagels getting showered with the stuff? Will eating the bagel, if it's covered with paint chips that have disguised themselves among the other crusted toppings, make me stupider?

Whatever.

My bagels are safe inside a paper bag. My pills are extra safe, wrapped in plastic and sealed in a bottle.

They're what matters most.

The New Normal makes me calculate everything in terms of the opportunity cost of going down and then back up these steps. If the bagels don't make it, or get compromised by lead paint chips, I'll be sad; if the pills don't make it, I'll be going back out again for more after a desperate phone call to one of my doctors to get my insurance to cover them. I desire the bagels; I need the pills.

I hate what this process is doing to me.

I hate how this process is making me feel.

Step five.

Step six.

Halfway there.

Time for another break.

My break this time is a little longer, a little more introspective, like the summer break between high school and college when you get to be proud of what you've accomplished, but know full well that there's more hard work ahead. I peek behind me at the steps I've already conquered, and ahead at the rest to come.

I wipe my forehead, crack my neck again, and bring the loop on the plastic bag back into alignment with the rest of the bag. That's futile, but I do it anyway.

I slide my right hand up the railing again, stepping with my good leg while unweighting from the crutch under my left armpit.

I miss.

I trip.

My good leg slips off the seventh step. My body pitches backward. I can't bring the crutches up in time to hold me, and my weight comes down on my bad leg.

The pain cuts me like a heavy, rusty serrated blade skewering my knee, the pain worse than any I've had in a while, and I've forgotten just how bad it could be. Still, I hold on, my right hand clamped to the railing, dragging myself forward.

Safe.

I slump there, my head against the railing, with a rope of drool running down my chin and fresh tears in my eyes, trying to catch my breath.

I saved myself on instinct, without even the time for panic, but now I had plenty for the fear, the dread, the paranoia that slips and trips like this produce in me. The worst is the fear that I'll break the other leg, that the other leg will break. I'll slide down the concrete steps like a boneless blob of jelly, maybe hitting my chin against each step on the way down until I'm lying flat on my back in the middle of the sidewalk, watching the pigeons peck at my bagels, which will have rolled out of the bag onto the street beside me.

I would swat at them, unless maybe I've broken one of my arms as well. Or, both of my arms.

There's a joke I heard in grade school about a guy walking along the beach who comes across a woman with no arms and legs who first wants to be held, so he holds her, and then wants to be kissed, so he kisses her, and then wants to be screwed, so he throws her in the ocean.

That would be me.

I hate the doubt, the fear, the cold, clammy paranoia that's overtaken me and given birth to The New Normal.

Maybe The New Normal isn't truly normal yet, because then I would have known better than to move my leg and my arm together; they are supposed to be separate, distinct movements, three points of contact with something secure at all times. Never move an arm and a leg in concert.

The roiling fear in my stomach of being the armless, legless drowning woman because I've tripped and fallen down my stoop subsides, and now I focus on the new pain.

Pain comes in 57 varieties, and right now I'm choking on most of them.

When I'm sitting still on my couch it's a steady throb, throbbing in time to my heartbeat— most people don't figure out that when something is throbbing, like waves crashing and receding and crashing and receding and crashing yet again, over and over, the throb is in time to their heartbeat— when the heart is clenched the throb is at its peak, when the systolic pressure relaxes into the diastolic calm, the pain lessens with it. Unless I move or disturb it somehow, then the baseline throbbing pain, The New Normal, spikes with a sharp, acute agony that always makes my breath catch, no matter how used to it I should be by now.

The painkillers smooth out and stretch out and hold down the waves of heartbeat throbbing, transforming it from a fast paced house beat played at top volume to something slower and mellower, some kind of 60's surf music or something; I should really do some research on that, what kind of music the pain feels like when the pills are in full effect; after all, I have nothing but time on my hands so I really could afford to spend a little while trying to figure out what kind of music the pain feels like when I'm dopy, but somehow I probably won't. The painkillers also make the acute pain less acute, hazier, foggier, and further away. Could I reinjure myself? Could I end up believing that I'm not really as damaged as I really am because it hurts less because of the pills, and I end up doing something I'm not physically ready for?

After I catch my breath, I straighten up.

I'm cautious, expecting the pain to ratchet up a little more, but it doesn't. For the moment, it's receded to a regular background throb, throbbing harder and worse than before I slipped, but not unbearably all-unifying.

I dropped my crutches; they're lying on the step beside me.

There's no prop guy waiting off stage to hand me new ones.

Very slowly, very deliberately, I turn towards them, grabbing onto the railing with both hands. Then I lower myself into a squat on my good leg, using the contracting quadriceps and my grip on the railing to control my descent, my bad leg jutting out to my side, and then I stretch out my left hand, grab the crutches, and pull myself back up, until I get the crutches beneath me.

I have two crutches, one for each arm, but I only use them both when I'm on flat ground; otherwise, I use only one, and the second one is fastened to the one I'm using with two Velcro straps my girlfriend rigged up for me when I demonstrated the problem.

Finished with this distracting, draining detour, I rotate back around, pause, get my grip on the railing reestablished, and climb up, paying more attention to where my good leg goes. There's nothing on the step itself that should have made my leg slip, but it had, and I'd almost taken a tumble.

I could have broken my other leg. But I didn't.

Step seven.

My girlfriend...

Was she coming to see me tonight? I'd made plans with her... right? Definitely, I'd talked to her earlier, I was pretty certain, but I was a little zonked on the pills, and I remember talking to her, but not what we'd decided.

I want to see her.

Is she happy with what The New Normal has done to our relationship? She can't be; I'm not, and I wouldn't blame her if she didn't want to see me tonight. Maybe she does want to see me tonight. Her natural instinct is to look forward to seeing me until she remembers what happened to me, what I'm like now, what The New Normal has done to me, and her interest in seeing me fades. Certainly, my interest in being myself fades every morning when I wake up and see what The New Normal has done to me.

The New Normal is having very unspontaneous sex with her on top, taking it easy; I like it and she seems to, but it's getting a little old for the both of us, and it lacks the springy, animalistic, passionate nature it's supposed to have; this is careful and weak and always distracted and, worse of all, planned, planned with logistics that must make her feel like an assistant instead of a lover. Once, a week or two ago, or maybe more, I can't quite remember, we were having sex and my girlfriend knocked into the contraption holding my knee together while the healing process ssssslowlyyyy takes place as the grafts and space age plastics and whatever else knit themselves together, one of her ass cheeks bumped into it and I screamed and lurched back in the bed and the two of us had a little moment there together, holding each other, the sex forgotten as the tentacles of The New Normal reached for her, too. We've only been together for a few months, and I wouldn't blame her if she didn't want to play wet nurse until I'm back together again.

All this thinking about sex adds a little pep to my step as I reach further up the railing for the next move.

I've got a bottle of KY in the bag, with the pills and the bagels. I've been jerking off like I'm a teenager again with an itch that I can't scratch, jerking off with more vigor than I can ever remember, like my body thinks it's dying and shooting off into a tissue is the only slim chance I've got to get my biology out there for the next generation. I heard that hanged men cum in their pants for the same reason. I don't know. Whoever told me that may have made it up. Whatever. It's the kind of thing I have all the time in the world to research, right after I figure out what kinds of music correspond to my pains, but I probably won't.

Step eight.

Step nine.

I'm going to get inside and take my pills and jerk off and then, finally, maybe eat one of my bagels unless I drift off, dissociate, obliviate, float away on a sea of cognitive dissonance, passing in and out of sleep without being aware of it, like hearing a noise and turning my head to investigate and then, sometime later, wondering 'Why is my head turned? Why have I been staring at the corner of the room like there's something there, but there isn't, when I'm really just trying to watch TV?' In which case, I'll eat my bagels when I return to consciousness later, even if they're a little stale by then.

Maybe my girlfriend'll have one, if she wants.

If she's coming to visit. Was she coming to see me tonight? I'd made plans with her... right? Definitely, I'd talked to her earlier, I was pretty certain, but I was a little zonked on the pills, and I remember talking to her, but not what we'd decided.

My left hand has a little ache to it.

I've got a blister.

Not the first time.

When I get inside, I'll have to carefully pop it; not squash it flat; instead, I'll poke two little holes at opposite ends of it and let the fluid inside weep out. After I take my pills but before I jerk off, and then, finally, maybe eat one of my bagels unless I drift off, dissociate, obliviate, float away on a sea of cognitive dissonance, passing in and out of sleep without being aware of it, like hearing a noise and turning my head to investigate and then, sometime later, wondering 'Why is my head turned? Why have I been staring at the corner of the room like there's something there, but there isn't, when I'm really just trying to watch

TV?' In which case, I'll eat my bagels when I return to consciousness later, even if they're a little stale by then.

Maybe my girlfriend'll have one, if she wants. If she's coming to visit.

Maybe I won't get all the pus out of the blister before I start jerking off. The fresh fluid will mix nicely with the KY. I'll have some kind of weird necrophiliac thing going, the pus and the KY mixing together, the fresh, baby soft skin under the blister nice and soft against my hard cock in my hand as I desperately bust into a tissue like the hanged men shooting off in their pants because it's their last chance. The soft skin under the blister won't hurt because the pills take care of all the hurt.

God, that's gross.

And pathetic.

I hate myself.

No, that's not true. I don't exactly hate myself. I hate my body. Which is me, obviously. In some fundamental way, but not exactly.

I hate my body like some poor girl misled into thinking she's fat and ugly, starving herself until she's nothing but skull and collarbones because of some model on a magazine cover. I watched a whole show on that, on one of those cable channels, the History Channel, learning channel, one of those channels that likes to pretend it's classier and above the fray, not appealing to the lowest common denominator while it does just that. The show followed a group of younger girls who were starving themselves. The show's shrink said that the real reason they starve themselves is that they have no control over anything in their lives but what they consume, that everything else is random except for the decision to eat that tiny sliver of fruit, or not. The shrink said that they don't hate themselves, after all. They hate having no control over anything in their lives but their diets, so that's where they clamp down the hardest, because they can.

But I hate my body.

For failing me.

My body failed me, worse than my car seizing up and leaving me at the side of an interstate in the middle of a thunderstorm in the middle of the night, or my phone dying during an important call. Those failures only seemed like failures until something as fundamental as my body failed me, revealing those other failures to be inconveniences, ignorantly, naively, innocently mislabeled as failures, because The New Normal has taught me the difference.

I'll get over all this once I get inside.

As soon as I get inside I'll take my pills, pop my blister and jerk off and by the time I'm done, instead of hating myself, I'll be looking forward to eating my bagels, unless I drift off, dissociate, obliviate, float away on a sea of cognitive dissonance, passing in and out of sleep without being aware of it, like hearing a noise and turning my head to investigate and then, sometime later, wondering 'Why is my head turned? Why have I been staring at the corner of the room like there's something there, but there isn't, when I'm really just trying to watch TV?' In which case, I'll eat my bagels when I return to consciousness later, even if they're a little stale by then.

But hating my body for failing me will definitely subside, especially if I treat myself to an extra half pill. If I call my girlfriend and she's not coming over, I could even treat myself to an extra whole pill, but that'll probably leave me passed out and drooling on my chest. At least I won't hate myself for having a body that failed me.

Step ten.

I haven't said a word about hating myself to my girlfriend. That wouldn't be fair, letting The New Normal envelop her too, trying to make her responsible for my despairing self-hatred.

I'd mentioned this to my physical therapist once or twice. A guy named Juan comes to my apartment two or three times a week. I find myself babbling to him as we slowly, slowly bend and flex the rubble in my knee after he takes the contraption off my leg. The exercises hurt, and I've cried a couple of times while working with him. He shrugs it off because the bromance that's brewing between us as he helps fold and unfold the damaged joint is strictly one-sided. I've made a few sarcastic remarks about how I wish fixing my knee was like changing a lightbulb or something, and all he did was laugh and say that he'd have to find another job if it were.

That was the closest to telling anyone how much the failure failed me. He asked me about the painkillers, if I was taking them correctly. I'd said that I had, and that was the truth. Still, The New Normal makes me secretive about things, keeps me from telling people that I hate myself and that I don't have to wonder how it would feel if I ate the entire bottle of pills all at once— it would feel great, I know it, and that's part of The New Normal as well, the knowledge that taking the entire bottle would just make me drift off faster and better than usual, and that instead of popping the blister I'd just float away and never come back and someone else would get the chance to eat my bagels.

Step eleven.

In the old days before The New Normal, I'd have my keys out already. I would have gotten them out while I was effortlessly climbing the stairs with a body that hadn't failed me, still foolishly believing that a dead cellphone qualified as a failure rather than an inconvenience, getting the front door key into my fingers and oriented the right way all by touch because the key is big and has a hexagonal shaped head, so all I would have to do is make sure the serrations were facing upward, which would be easy because my sense of touch and feeling would be free to make such a simple exploration with ease, because my sense of touch and feeling wouldn't be dominated by all the different categories of pain the way Inuits have hundreds of names for snow because of how much of a role it plays in their lives.

But The New Normal has turned getting the keys out of my pants into its own procedure to be performed only when I'm holding onto the solid brass doorknob of the building, since otherwise I could drop my crutches. Then I could fall and break the other leg while I attempt to retrieve them.

If I broke the other leg, I'd need a wheelchair. I'd be living in a hospital somewhere, hoping that someone would help me get to the toilet on time instead of dealing with those few inches of free-fall between the end of my quadriceps contraction and the bowl. If I broke the other leg, I'd hate myself even more. Probably someone else would be feeding me my painkillers. I'd have no chance to take extras as a reward for sitting on my couch because my girlfriend wasn't coming to visit because she didn't want to ride me anymore with caution.

But I haven't broken my other leg, at least not yet.

Is that optimism? Or, am I just preaching to myself? Have I turned into my own infomercial positivity evangelist because I've established a New Normal instead of just hitting rock bottom and wallowing there?

The New Normal has transformed optimism about my future— getting a raise, getting married, moving to a nicer place— into a grim determination to tolerate things getting worse. If I can take this failure without completely breaking, then I can take others, right? If this is the New Normal, then aren't there other New Normals that I haven't had to contend with? Doesn't that mean that I am coping with this one?

Step twelve.

I grasp the doorknob to the building and smell the garlic from the bagels; there's still moisture carrying the smell to me, which means that they haven't started going stale yet. I get my keys out.

I get my key into the lock, push the door open, and hobble inside, leaning against the wall as I pull apart my crutches so I can use both to get to my apartment at the end of the hall.

I'll pop the blister, jerk off, eat my bagels, and call my girlfriend, and then, only then, will I allow myself to take one of the pills.

Maybe I'll only take half.

Brendan Praniewicz earned his MFA in creative writing from San Diego State in 2007 and has subsequently taught creative writing at San Diego colleges. He has had poetry published in *From Whispers to Roars, Tiny Seed Journal, That Literary Review*, and *The Dallas Review.* In addition, he received second place in a first-chapters competition in the *Seven Hills Review* Chapter Competition in 2019. He won first place in The

Rilla Askew Short Fiction Contest in 2020. He was a 2023 Pushcart Nominee for poetry. He can be found on Facebook (Brendan Praniewicz), Instagram (@praniewicz), and his website is brendan-praniewicz.com

The Devil

On a promising Friday afternoon, Darius and Jocelyn traveled to the San Diego County Fair. A faint, coastal breeze did little to temper the relentless, dry August heat. But they came prepared, lathered in oily sunscreen and adorned in summer attire—shorts, tees, and flipflops. They nibbled on cheese fries as they perused past vendors. Darius munched on soft-drink ice while Jocelyn oohed and aahed at the adorable baby animals and the abundance of fried food. Children screamed on janky rides while the air filled with aromas of funnel cake and powdered sugar. They strolled closely together, not touching or holding hands, but closer than they had in some time.

Jocelyn clutched a teddy bear that Darius won at a game of ring toss. Her pink t-shirt stretched over her stomach. Two months pregnant, she felt her belly begin to swell like a waxing strawberry moon. Her dark hair, gathered in a ponytail, accentuated her oval face, flush cheeks, and chestnut eyes—she looked stunning as always. The fair brought a sense of needed escape and adventure. Their marriage held so much uncertainty, but the promise of a child had cooled many disputes.

Passing a tarot card reader, Jocelyn's eyes lit up as she tugged Darius' arm.

"Let's get our fortunes taken," she said.

Darius reluctantly agreed.

Tarot cards stirred Bostonian memories—poached eggs, Egyptian coffee, and breakfast with his mother. A bohemian at heart, she performed tarot readings every morning at the kitchen table when he was a child. Eyebrows furrowed, she'd speak in a theatrical New England dialect and attempt to predict the day's events, which rarely came true. Darius found it all absurd and hokey. He never shared these memories with Jocelyn because his childhood embarrassed him.

As Jocelyn and Darius approached the booth, a fortune teller, with cropped auburn hair and a deep scar over her eyebrow, greeted them in a soft voice and introduced herself as Cassandra. Her pale wrists held gaudy bracelets with moon-shaped charms. A silver owl pendant hung from her necklace, reminding Darius of his mother, who loved these mythical, feathered creatures. His mother had owl ornaments and knick-knacks in every cupboard and bookshelf of his boyhood home. After introducing herself, Cassandra led them to a candlelit room, lined with dark curtains. To Darius' surprise, Jocelyn nestled next to him.

She held his hand as they gathered at a small pub table and awaited their fortunes.

A black candle flickered on the table while Cassandra settled before them and shuffled a pack of cards with her stubby fingers. But one card jumped out of the deck and landed on the ground beside Darius.

He glanced down, and beside his flip-flop lay the Devil. Satan, clearly a bad omen on an auspicious day, was the last thing he needed. He placed his foot over the card and hoped no one noticed.

But Cassandra saw everything. Ducking under the table, she scurried around for a bit, determined to find the card. She brushed Darius' foot aside and brought the Devil into the light.

"I'll put this one back in the pack," Cassandra said.

Darius huffed in relief, hoping she wouldn't conjure the Devil again. But Cassandra didn't return it. Instead, she paused to study the card while she peered at Darius.

"No," Cassandra said, setting the Devil on the table. "This card belongs to you."

Jocelyn released Darius' hand. She nodded with conviction as if she knew her husband was the Devil all along.

Darius wiped sweat from his forehead and stared in disbelief. Of all the 72 cards in that deck, it had to be this one. What were the odds? He had a history with the Devil, a frequent guest at his mother's table, and her words and interpretations came to life.

The Devil—Baphonet—the horned goat of Mendes—a scapegoat for all things evil.

The Devil represented one's shadow side.

The Devil signified instant gratification and sexual cravings.

His mother often told him, when placed upright, Baphonet stood for darkness. But when positioned upside down, the meaning is reversed, rendering the opposite: discipline, restraint, and sobriety. But in this moment, the Devil lay upright, demonic eyes glaring into Darius.

"It's not a bad card," Cassandra tried to mitigate his misfortune, while Jocelyn, completely irritated, crossed her arms. "He means well," the fortune teller continued. "He likes to lie and hide to avoid hurting others. He's a deceiver with good intentions."

Cassandra's words, designed to soften the tension, fired straight into Jocelyn's heart. Somehow, perhaps through luck or pure black magic, Cassandra had summoned the most divisive and traumatic issue in their marriage. Jocelyn's face and neck reddened while she stood and slung her purse over her shoulder.

"I'm leaving," she said and rushed out of the room.

Cassandra, surprised, bit her lip and shoved the Devil back into the deck. Darius, humiliated, apologized and handed her twenty-five dollars.

With a teddy bear tucked under his arm, Darius raced through the fairgrounds and dodged crowds of people. Reaching Jocelyn, he tapped her shoulder.

"We shouldn't be together," she said with her head down, plowing forward.

On the ride home, the air conditioner blasted through dusty vents, but the car never cooled down. Country music softly crooned from speakers while Darius drove down the 5 Freeway. Haunted by Cassandra's words, he gazed through the bug-pelted windshield, where rocky coastline stretched for miles. In the passenger's seat, Jocelyn rubbed her belly counterclockwise. She repeated the same words over and over as if casting a spell—they weren't meant to be together.

Two years into his marriage, Darius experienced one of the most embarrassing and painful days of his life when he drove home from work on a Friday afternoon, hoping to spend a peaceful weekend with his wife. He found Jocelyn in their home office, standing before the computer. She held a bank statement in her trembling fingers.

"What's going on?" Darius asked.

"I found your receipts."

"For what?"

"For the two thousand dollars you spent on webcam girls."

On this day, Jocelyn discovered her husband was the Devil.

Darius, stunned and speechless, sank into a chair and rubbed his forehead. Judgment day had arrived, a digital crime scene lay before him, and Darius simmered in hell. When they married, they agreed to split bank accounts and share bills to avoid disputes. At the time, Darius had nothing to hide, but recently, he developed a proclivity for nude cam shows. A betrayal happened here. Jocelyn stood over him, and she clung to the statement in her hands while her sad, brown eyes searched for answers.

A lifelong, traumatic journey brought Darius into this moment. As a child, he became sexually charged and precocious after losing his innocence. Molested by a church youth group leader in middle school had tarnished him. When his parents found out, his father and mother fought more, and a year later, they divorced. Darius blamed himself for everything. He should've known better. He should've been smarter. If only he were stronger. Had he not been sexually abused, Darius believed his parents would have stayed together. These tragedies didn't make him a bad apple, but a bruised one.

In his freshman year of high school, Darius found something that would change his life—smutty magazines. Entering puberty and hyper sexual, Darius was drawn to lewd photos that garnered his curiosity. Sex terrified him, but in these glossy pages, he found a safe place to explore unanswered questions. But these discoveries also brought guilt and humiliation—sex, for Darius, originated in shame. When the internet entered his home in the late 90s, porn went from hard-to-find magazines to instant downloads in his bedroom. His high school classmates turned to drugs and alcohol, but Darius escaped into pixilated nudity. With time, porn became an uncontrollable obsession, one that isolated him and left him feeling perverted. Pleasure and shame fueled his cognitive dissonance—desiring something but feeling guilty when receiving it—the root of all addiction. The Devil's appetite feasted on shame.

Jocelyn knew he watched porn, but not to the extent, and Darius didn't explore webcams until recently. That summer, he began searching adult sites for webcam models who lived in far-off countries, and they seduced him into private shows with salacious teasing and touching. Darius never went cam-to-cam—no woman ever saw him. And his lustful behavior was provoked by recent turmoil. Graduating college during the Great Recession, he struggled to find work. He took a high-risk sales job, an occupation he had no knowledge of or experience in, and his boss constantly threatened to fire him if Darius didn't meet quotas. And that spring, his mother died in a car accident, leaving him with endless grief. Jocelyn, fearful of losing her job during a recession, worked 12-hour days and came home exhausted. Darius, alone and depressed, turned to the internet to numb his pain.

And this long, twisted history—the Devil's blueprint—brought Darius into the present, this altercation with his wife. He sank deeper into the stiff office chair. An assortment of empty coffee mugs and wedding photos spread across the computer desk—the scene where Darius committed his transgressions. Through the window, the sun gradually descended behind apartment complexes. The office grew dimmer. Darius blamed himself—his past didn't excuse his behaviors. He, an adult, chose to waste money on transitory fantasies. And worst of all, he brought his wife into this underworld. Jocelyn stood before him, her shoulders backlit by the computer's red screen saver. She whispered numbers from the statement and shook her head in disbelief.

"This is cheating," she said.

"I'm sorry," Darius sank his face into the shadows.

Jocelyn said nothing else. She set the statement down, took her phone to the bedroom, and locked the door.

Darius, filled with shame, rocked back and forth in the chair. Part of him still believed that his molestation caused his parents' divorce, and now, his sexual perversion ruined his marriage. He was a monster. No, Darius was the Devil. Jocelyn had every right to leave him. She deserved better, and he deserved what came.

The next morning, Darius woke up on the couch. He slept in his clothes, and a small Afghan blanket covered his shoulders and torso. Opening his eyes, he scanned the living room and expected to find packed suitcases and a farewell letter. Instead, he discovered Jocelyn, standing in the kitchen. With her back turned to him, she prepared a salad.

Standing, Darius rubbed his eyes and gathered his words while his bare feet pressed against cold tile.

He approached her and said, "I'm sorry for what I did, and I'll do whatever it takes to fix all of this."

Jocelyn said nothing. She shoved her lunch in a brown bag, brushed past him, and left for work.

The next month fell into drudgery and constant bickering. But Darius, through pleading and costly gifts, persuaded his wife to stay, even though she veered toward divorce. To uphold his commitment to change, Darius attended weekly therapy sessions and worked on past trauma. He joined a porn addicts anonymous group and went to meetings three times a week. Through step work and service, he learned strategies to combat his compulsive behaviors. Lastly, he installed accountability software on his computer so his wife would receive reports of everything he watched online.

Jocelyn, raised religiously, decided that after discovering Darius' secret, she'd return to church. Only God could provide answers, through her prayers, on how to mend their marital disharmony. Darius was happy his wife sought spiritual consultation, but when she encouraged him to join her, he resisted. The last time he stepped into a parish was the day the youth group leader molested him. If going to church meant saving his marriage, Darius had limits—he couldn't sell out his inner child.

Darius never watched webcam girls again. But freeing himself from porn remained a barrier. Occasionally, when overstressed or when his emotions ran wild, he'd slip into a porn binge. But this rarely happened, maybe every two months, which was still progress for him, going from viewing it every day. But his momentary regressions angered and disappointed Jocelyn. Wasn't she attractive? Wasn't she enough? How many Bible verses speak against coveting and adultery? Most of all, Jocelyn feared that his porn use would lead him into the temptation of webcam models, or worse, an affair with a coworker or someone else. Trust had been broken, wounds remained open; impossible to heal.

A year after the "discovery," Darius took sales calls in his office on a warm summer day, when Jocelyn texted him. She never messaged him at work, and he wondered if he'd done something wrong. His last porn episode was a month ago, and since then, he hadn't done anything to upset her. He opened the text and found a blurry photo of something that resembled a thermometer. Darius enlarged the picture as Jocelyn sent another message—*I'm pregnant.*

A sense of joy overcame him, and he called her right away.

"I'm so happy," he said.

"Me too."

"I love you so much, Jocelyn. You're going to be the best mother ever."

The pregnancy brought new focus, expectations, and vigor. Jocelyn dreamed of motherhood, and her gift had arrived. For Darius, the baby brought a sense of renewal. More than a year had passed since his mother died, and she would've called this "celestial timing," meaning the pregnancy fulfilled the circle of death and birth.

Even though problems lurked in their marriage, Jocelyn and Darius had endured a recession, a near divorce, and the loss of his mother. Together, they grew emboldened, battle-tested, and ready for parenthood.

Jocelyn kept the pregnancy a secret from friends and family in case of any early complications. But with every passing week, she leaked the secret to her loved ones. Over the next two months, Darius and Jocelyn went from marital collapse to planning baby showers, choosing bedroom colors, and searching for a bigger apartment.

Two months later, they had visited Cassandra, the tarot card reader, and the surprising reveal of the Devil card had reignited trust issues in their marriage. Two days after the reading, Darius slipped into porn—the first time since Jocelyn became pregnant. Turmoil returned. But the catalyst for his relapse was his mother's upcoming birthday, which landed on the last day of August. Between the Devil and memories of his mother, Darius escaped into the familiar.

To mend the situation, he planned a day trip to the Getty Museum with Jocelyn for Labor Day weekend. The drive there was quiet. Jocelyn scrolled on her phone while Darius hummed to Led Zeppelin songs—his mother's favorite band.

The Getty Museum, on a beautiful September afternoon, had a way of alleviating tension. Far from the trials of home and work, Darius and Jocelyn experienced reprieve as they sipped sparkling water. They gazed over museum terraces, offering vistas of Bel Air mansions and nearby mountains. In the distance, downtown Los Angeles rose from earth and concrete, and on this day, smog had lifted, revealing a placid ocean. Together they wandered through galleries of enchanting artwork. Darius lingered in a

Monet exhibit and became entranced by sunlight reflecting off of waterscapes. His mother favored the Impressionists, and to commemorate her birthday, Darius immersed himself in what she loved.

Halfway through the tour, Jocelyn became ill and rushed to the bathroom. Darius waited by a life-size painting of the Sun King, Louis XIV.

Twenty minutes later, Jocelyn returned. Her eyes flooded with tears, and she trembled as if she had just escaped some haunted place.

"What's wrong?" Darius asked, hurrying to her.

"The baby's dead."

She had a miscarriage in the bathroom. Darius wrapped her in his arms. Jocelyn wept into his shoulder. Patrons strolled by, some observing and even taking photos as if Jocelyn and Darius were a performance art piece, representing suffering. Jocelyn lost her baby.

For Darius, the child died a day after his mother's birthday.

The next day, Darius drove Jocelyn to the hospital for a checkup after the miscarriage. In the passenger's seat, his wife wore sweats and no makeup. Tears streamed down her cheeks. Darius pressed dark sunglasses to his face to conceal his sadness.

He held her hand as he guided the car through morning traffic. Jocelyn's stiff fingers felt corpse cold, as if the miscarriage had killed her too.

"This wasn't meant to be," she said.

"What? The baby?"

"No, us."

"What do you mean?"

"I should've never married you. You're a liar who hides secrets from his wife."

He absorbed her words, sank in the seat, and focused on brake lights.

Jocelyn continued, "This miscarriage is just more proof that God doesn't want us together. He took our child because of you."

Dreams were shattered at the Getty. They lost their baby in Bel Air, the embodiment of American success, and were left feeling like failures. Their child —the only bond holding their marriage together. Everything Jocelyn ever wanted disappeared in a bathroom stall. Frustration, despair, and fury, she voiced all of these emotions and rightfully so. Darius bit his lower lip and listened. This was a mother's moment, not his. He steered through congested traffic and thought about his stepsister, who had five miscarriages before delivering her first child. Each one was more devastating than the last. Losing a child brought every shade of hell.

Darius gazed beyond a small crack in the windshield. Above the 8 Freeway, sunlight brushed the edges of gray clouds. Miscarriages were an unfortunate part of having a child, but it didn't mean they weren't meant to be together. Jocelyn placed death on him, for being dishonest, a poor choice for a husband, and because of this, God denied them a family. Behind dark sunglasses, Darius thought about people who had murdered, who had raped, who had committed serial adultery—some of the worst men in history fathered children. It was equivalent to blaming hurricanes and earthquakes on human immorality. Nothing Darius had ever done resulted in the death of their child.

Beside him, Jocelyn's sobs grew louder. He offered warmth by rubbing her cold hand. Darius loved her, and he wished for the power to remove her pain.

Before him, clouds rolled forward, blotting out the sun. His shame returned—the one emotion that governed him. He had a history of ruining relationships, from his parents' marriage to his own. Positioned in the driver's seat, he had responsibility in this. He should've never begged Jocelyn to stay when she insisted on leaving him. He had denied the truth—after what had happened, she would never forgive or accept him. Had he let her go, Jocelyn would've never become pregnant. The baby would've never lived or died. Suffering would've never transpired.

The mark of Cain had been set on him long ago, not scarred in flesh, but carved deep in the chambers of his heart. Darius needed no one to convince him—he was the Devil.

Kenneth M. Kapp lives with his wife in Milwaukee, Wisconsin, writing late at night in his man-cave. He enjoys chamber music and mysteries. He has been nominated for the Pushcart Prize. His stories have appeared in more than ninety publications worldwide, including the *Saturday Evening Post, October Hill Magazine, EgoPHobia* in Romania, *Lothlorien Poetry Journal* in Ireland, and *The Wise Owl* in India.

I Heard It

I hear better with my eyes closed; better still if I can move with the sounds. My one passion: Chamber Music. I taught mathematics at an urban university where a world-famous string quartet was in residence, offering several recitals each year. Heaven was across the school's quadrangle. However, the music was theirs and Beethoven, or theirs and Mozart. Not mine. One day, when I was returning to my office from the Student Union, in the middle of a public street that cuts through the university, I heard it, a quartet that filled my head with sounds, sounds all my own.

Minerva Laveaga Luna is a storyteller, editor, and translator. She is the recipient of the 2026 PEN American Bare/Life Review Grant. Her hybrid essay "The Day of the Dead" was a finalist for the 2025 *American Literary Review* Nonfiction Contest. Her work is anthologized in *Con la urgencia del instante* (2023, Ars Cumminis) and *Borderlines (2015, Voices Breaking Boundaries)*. Her work has appeared in *Atticus Review, Rio Grande Review*, and *Southwestern American Literature*. She is an alum of Tin House, *The Kenyon Review*, and

Macondo Writers' residential workshops. Formerly the Director and subsequent Board President of the literary nonprofit organization BorderSenses, she co-founded the literary press Veliz Books. Minerva earned a B.A. in Philosophy and an MFA from UTEP. She is an English Professor at El Paso Community College.

A Lime

The road turns around hills as if pushed by the car's headlights. My eyes follow the white lines that shine in the dark. I am training. With time, I will appreciate and look for swirling paths. My brothers sleep next to me in the back seat. My parents are quiet in the front, all of us sinking into the night with Serrat, Javier Solis, and The Beatles playing on the stereo.

I know this stretch. We go back and forth between Mexico City and Durango in the years before we finally move to Durango when I'm ten years old. This part of the road looks familiar, yet I don't recall ever noticing the house perched on a hill when we turn. The light from the window whispers warmth. Its distant glow snuggled between hills and trees. I think Urgl and Engywook from *The Never-Ending Story* could live here.

"If they don't have anything else, ask them to at least give you a lime," my mom tells my dad as he gets out of the car. We are parked in a small clearing by the hill. Semis loaded with wood rattle us when they pass by. I feel like the universe, with all its movements, is against me. I think of the winding road still ahead, the earth moving around the sun, rotating, and I find myself closer to getting sick. Awoken by the sudden stop, my brothers ask what we are doing there. I ask if I can get out, but my mom says we are too close to the road, and it's too dark. I wonder if the people in the house can see us from their window. My dad must be gesturing toward the car, describing his little girl, who suffers from motion sickness. I roll down my window, but the air is too cold up in the mountains, so I close it.

When my dad returns, he has a lime. I take it, peel a tiny circle with my small fingers, and inhale the healing smell that calms my stomach. "We are almost to the point where the road stops turning," he says, starting the engine. I know he is only talking to me. He wants me to believe I cannot feel nauseous if the road is straight. The Beatles finish the line I interrupted when I said I was going to be sick. Aware that I've already delayed us, I fight the impulse to turn back as the car begins to move. Any movement, especially turning, would undo the lime's work. I only imagine the house and its window getting smaller. I don't know that I will search for its light on countless other roads, far from here.

Claire Low, also known as Claire Engkaninan Low, is a Sydney-based artist and writer who lives on Cammeraygal land. She is a former newspaper journalist and magazine editor. As a horror writer, her work is published in Australia by Clan Destine Press and in America, by Castle Bridge Media. She was an Australasian Shadows Award nominee for her novelette published in This Fresh Hell. As an artist, her most acclaimed works have a sustainability focus and reimagine used materials. clairelow.com

Material

Oniomania sounds Greek and tragic. The word for compulsive buying disorder sounds like a problem for literary heroines, or an out-of-body experience. It wasn't me, it was the oniomania. The monster whispering in my ear, '*this will complete you, this will make you worth something*', has a name.

I bought things when I was happy and when I was sad; when I felt accomplished, and when I didn't. Cheap things, expensive things. I wanted to say things about myself, like a London It-girl, I love Mulberry. Like a tanned socialite on Corfu, I have a Pucci scarf. I could say these things to myself while actually being a suburban Canberran who, up until recently, loved the $11 rack at Tree of Life.

I shopped for Australian designer fashion because I wanted to say, 'Please believe I am a credible fashion writer. I spent so much on a used Chloe handbag that the bank rang. And at Australian Fashion Week, I shifted it toward street-style photographers, like a sunflower seeking the light. Please believe I belong here. But $900 of oxblood leather did not make me more interesting and failed to cure my hunger for more.

I felt an undercurrent of disgust and tried to squash it by going to sale-bargain bins, petting more English-made leather, and ordering another piece from Nordstrom. I was not alone: the endless swipe of a credit card is as Australian as a democracy sausage. Per ASIC's report 580, ***Credit Card Lending in Australia***, there's a deluge of debt: its snapshot of the credit card market found $31.7 billion in balances on cards being charged interest. It's an everyday angst.

I felt a thrill when each object arrived, inhaled its rich aromas, and got high on the life it promised. But I was already chasing the next new thing.

When Rana Plaza collapsed, taking with it more than 1300 garment workers' lives, I felt the Made in Bangladesh tags on my clothes turn blood red. Thirty-eight murder charges were brought in that large-scale industrial disaster, and I realised the cost of my cheap clothes had been much too high.

Women keened in the rubble, holding pictures of missing family, and I knew I hadn't bought those pieces because I loved them or even liked them that much, but because they were there. I had filled my time with them like people strolling into Primark in their lunch hour.

Sometimes, a *cri de coeur* has been sewn into a garment's label in neat stitches: DEGRADING SWEATSHOP CONDITIONS. Two British shoppers found messages; the second one said

FORCED TO WORK EXHAUSTING HOURS. The origin of the labels is unknown: guerrilla warfare in the change rooms with needle and thread? Insider job? Either is believable – how do you find time to sew a protest when forced to work exhausting, degrading hours? An anonymous retail executive told *The Guardian* that shoppers prefer cheap things over respect for human rights. And from the same source, a shifting of blame onto the tight-fisted consumer. "If you buy a pair of jeans at $9.99, what are you really expecting?"

"If you buy these things," former op shop manager Grace Meyer Jones says, "You're putting your lifestyle above someone else's life." Her green jumper is threadbare at the elbows; it was a discard from her workplace, considered unsalable. She wears it well. "[Workers] will lose their eyesight early because you wanted something beaded. Something sequined probably used child labour. To buy these things, you're trampling on women."

Those trampled-on women, Rana Plaza's surviving workers, still cry over their families that never came home, over human remains that might not have been that of their own loved ones, over the need to survive that drives them back to work at other garment factories, quite close to where the building fell. And fast fashion sells in a time of stagnant wage growth, while Instagram fuels a hunger for cheap trends; and TikTok influencers buy cartloads of clothes off shamefully cheap websites, blindfolded, for clicks and giggles.

The one thing that can make us care? Bodily horror. Like a grotesque fairytale, the rat story sticks out in my mind. A rat was sewn into the hem of a Manhattan woman's dress. Like a miniature Steven King monster, it spread terror among fast fashion lovers in my office.

The facts unfold with the slow build of a Hitchcock movie: she put on the dress. Went to work. Smelled a pungent odour, source unknown.

Felt a string brush against her leg. And it was not a string, but a dead rat's limb. The rest of its body was hidden in the hem. And then: an overwhelming desire to remove the dress, and later – allegedly – a rodent-borne disease. Zara needs only one week to develop new products and get them to stores; it launches thousands of products per year. The rat dress might be the most iconic one of all.

The terror comes from the feeling that it could have been any one of us, any office worker in the world. Perhaps one rat is worth ten factory collapses. One draws a sigh, a shake of the head, and the other elicits a shiver that never disappears.

At the end of my own Zara days, when I relaxed into being who I really am – not a high fashion socialite, more an approximation of me at 17 – I found myself enthralled by the world's largest exporter of cool. That would be Bella McFadden, 'InternetGirl', a grown-up Wednesday Adams with a Victoria's Secret body. Her talent for flipping used clothing is so big that she sits atop the world, the number one thrifter who can parlay rags into riches. She made enough money to propel herself from a Canadian prairie town to a Los Angeles loft. How does one dream girl raise herself to the top of Depop? (Imagine Instagram, only everything's for sale on a consumer-to-consumer app.) I'd say it's love and envy. We adore her. Her actual lover responds to pictures of her with the deranged smiley face; he's out of his mind about her. But we all are. She posts a picture with a Sailor Moon fringe and white fake talons poking into her flawless cheeks.

Someone begs her to slit their throat with those nails. Which is how you relate to celebrities these days. Looking at her makes our hearts squeeze covetously, like they do at the fake sparkle of Austrian crystal, carnival teddy bears, and glazed cherries on white cakes. The things we buy from her she calls 'trashion'; we receive them and say we're blessed, as though handed holy relics. That's a kind of love. The envy: we would also like to have a tall, slender body, pale and tattooed. Evelyn Waugh wrote that siblings are the same ingredients, differently dispensed. Bella's sister, Francesca, is a pageant princess with blonde hair like buttercream frosting. That same cherry pie wholesomeness that clashes with Bella's mallgoth subversiveness. Her sister reveals that underneath the tattoos and jelly bands, there's a fantasy woman. Told you: it's love and envy.

There's a glow around her as she walks down LA boulevards, the patron saint of thrift stores, making us crave things that others threw away. She makes us crazy as we try to steal her élan. We cross black hair ties over our wrists like the jelly bands she sells. Used is cool; all hail the op shop.

This means secondhand stores can open a gaping maw, swallow us whole. Preoccupy our waking hours, make our hearts race. We want this black slip, that achingly '00s skirt with tiny florals over mesh, those Lucite heels tall enough to shatter an ankle.

I go to those shops with rosaries and crucifixes under scratched glass countertops, with dubious watches, jade-green beads, and mysterious things. In the window: a crystal bowl, an antique chair, a stiff vintage dress, yellowed pearls. As though to cultivate the sweet, delusional idea a place like this is fancy, instead of the last stop, one final chance before the endgame of clothing – landfill. That's where much of it will go – into the ground with other waste, like the plastic we feel so bad about.

Each thrift store is full of ghosts. Clothes often hold the shape of their old owners; even worse, some are still new. Sifting the racks like a gold prospector, I'm struck by the intimacy of unwashed things, your shame, your secrets, things you shucked off your body, dresses that made you loathe yourself a little.

I have felt the place under which your heart beats. Your fashion mistakes, your breakup outfits, the shirts you dumped when your man moved out. I know your perfume and fabric softener. I've seen the stains under your arms; the fake fingernails you tucked into your purse; your missing 10c coin. I've absorbed your regret at the money you wasted; the big ache under it all.

The regret is bigger by the day. Clothing in Australia is wasted by the ton, and this is before you factor in the massive quantities of water it takes to grow cotton, carcinogenic chemicals in indigo dye, and poorly fed women sewing tough thread through. And every day, there are more shirts and jeans, and another poolside influencer spruiking brands that shed microplastics into the ocean with every wash of an inadequate synthetic bikini. Put a fingertip to those stretchy fabrics that show your skin right through, those poly-blends that look like garbage even brand new. About 10kg of dumped clothes per person ends up in the landfill each year, yet Shein still lures us with awfully cheap prices.

Awfully cheap, awfully exploitative, and an environmental disaster. But cheap.

Meyer Jones estimates that 60 percent of donations to her store never made it to the floor; there was no hope (sacks of dirty underwear; donations people literally sped away from). Of the 40 percent that was saleable, 80 percent probably made it out the door with a new owner.

The rest? Destined for a ragging company, but she notes with a touch of cynicism, that was regardless of whether things would have made good rags. When clothes were essentially plastic, there was no chance.

Practically speaking, what is there to be done? For Graham Ross of BlockTexx, who dreams of his marvellous machines at laundromats and music festivals, churning and turning unwanted textiles back into raw materials for use in many industries, we just need to recycle clothes with the same ardor we find for plastic. "It's almost as though we as human beings care more about a plastic bottle than our favourite T-shirt. You wouldn't leave a plastic bottle lying in the ground, but we throw clothing into landfills like it's nothing." His research found that the average garment in Australia is destined for just six uses, that globally about 75 million tons of PET are manufactured each year, and that about 50 million tons – two-thirds of it – goes into clothing and textiles. "Less than a third of it goes into plastic containers and bottles we feel so compelled to recycle. Two-thirds of that PET is in our clothing, and we don't have effective recycling systems for it globally." As for me, I love clothes and want others to love them too. In fact, some designers wonder if they can fight wastage by creating garments people love more, if only they design pieces that make us feel 'enclothed cognition', basically 'when your outsides match your insides'.

Searching for this feeling for other people, I match-make clothes. I want people to say yes to a dress (a pair of shoes, a tapestry handbag, a skirt). The money I make is modest, the environmental benefits negligible, like daintily skimming an oil spill out of the deep blue with a pipette. But I try. The clothes are sold to buyers worldwide. Authentically scavenged items, real fixer-uppers, sometimes with this season's high heel rip right through the hem.

One Chatswood thrift store is a magnet for special things. Go to the shoe area, flip over an architectural pair of shoes – chartreuse, deceptively simple, and find the name of a Belgian designer. The name sits oddly in a mouth used to broad, flat syllables: Dries van Noten. The price: $12. You sell these shoes to a dark-haired Manhattan photographer, and off they go to march around on her accomplished feet at art parties. You make a small sum. The shoes get a new life, and the op shop gets $12. That's the service. The same me who wanted a new designer handbag every month is scooping up clothes by the kilogram to try to save them.

Critics would say I'm gentrifying the op shops. Still, there is so much clothing everywhere, designer brands, all the rest of it, lying in Sydney's streets at council clean up—people couldn't even be bothered dragging it to Vinnies. Apparently, we have enough clothing for the next six generations. And as Anya Hindmarch says— she of the famous stampedecausing 'I'm not a plastic bag' totes—if we throw something away, there is *no away*.

The biggest place for sourcing items to send onto new lives, I call 'the ground sale'.

Everything was heaped in piles on tarpaulins. Shoppers crawl around in the clothes like flies on

Aeroplane Jelly. It doesn't matter whether something has Italian fabrics or is Australian-made by which label or whether it's a lousy rag from the most exploitative factory on earth, for they are all swirled together in a dreadful rainbow. Anything you care to buy can easily look like garbage. And somehow, out of this pile came a pristine white dress, the kind you'd see on a duchess: neat waist, shining perfection, everyone's black soles missed it. I sold it for enough money to cover the cost of all 40 pieces I bought that day, to Hong Kong, so while it narrowly missed the landfill, it cost a lot in carbon emissions on its flight over. It's hard to win.

When I sleep, I dream of collapsing Bangladeshi factories. Burberry goods, made by artisans, disappearing into smoke like a witch on a pyre, because even the cut-glass cheekbones of a tousle-haired model weren't enough to sell stock. They burn them because they don't want the goods to fall into the 'wrong' hands. Those handbags were supposed to hang from the arms of office workers in glass-front buildings; instead, they'll turn into air pollution, ash, then nothing.

Imagine sewing for a living: maybe on the outskirts of Seoul, where machines generate so much heat, there's a haze in the sky. Or in Bangladesh or Honduras. Imagine getting the long, slow futility of sewing things that will get buried in the ground. Do you feel this futility or, after all this time, feel nothing at all?

As the fashion cycle gets shorter and the desire for new things gets more feverish, even if you never see the ads, you know. The time between something appearing on a bus shelter on a carefully selected model, a glorious shade of brown, so a company meets its diversity goals, and the time when the garment is discarded, is a tiny slice of time. So small, you wonder why the model was asked to smile.

Joseph Byrd is a 2025 Best Small Fictions winner, a Pushcart Prize and Best of the Net nominee, and was in the StoryBoard Chicago cohort with Kaveh Akbar. An Associate Artist in Poetry under Joy Harjo at the Atlantic Center for the Arts, his work has appeared or is forthcoming in *West Trade Review*, *Exposition Review*, *The South Carolina Review*, *Stone Canoe*, *CutBank*, *Pedestal*, *South Florida Poetry Journal*, *DIAGRAM*, *Novus Literary Arts*, and elsewhere.

On Anger

If it had been mine, I'd have kept it. Anger loves a keeper the way a garden loves a hoe, aching to be tended. But it wasn't mine, even though I didn't know that then, or feel it, until that trip in the truck to the ponds south of Salem, our fishing poles in the back and some dumb sandwiches sprawled between my Dad and me as we drove, thankfully surrounded by the whiz of road noise that cauterized our conversation.

Dad didn't have a Dad. The lone, fading Polaroid masking taped to the Frigidaire of him with Grandpa Byrd's arm draped over Dad's four-year-old shoulders showed his blonde hair and his scared little grin framed by an Oklahoma sunrise as he leaned into a father he didn't know he'd never see again.

Decades later, while cleaning out Grandma's trailer after her death, Dad would find a yellowing stack of rubber-banded letters from his father, hand-scrawled missives she'd hidden from Dad, begging for a picture of their son. He also discovered that his Dad had lived an hour away from him his entire life, and had died a year before Grandma did.

Dad walked a lot after she died, wordless and returning to the house after hours of being somewhere else. I remember greeting him at the door, or trying to. He didn't want me near him most of the time while growing up, but especially not after his mother died.

Anger isn't an obvious thing when it grows. It's like St Augustine grass, with its stolons, those above-ground runners that form a spongy carpet above the dirt itself, keeping most of the grass from having contact with the loam below. My parents came from angry people, and they did their best to keep us from anger itself. But just like anything you try not to be, it's pretty easy for you to end up becoming it.

On that fishing trip, for reasons I still don't understand, something shifted, like a rock that slipped from a cliff face. That whole day, Dad was nice, an awful word hailing from a city in France where the fabric of Nice is crafted so finely, nothing can touch it that doesn't snag on it. Dad's niceness helped me see how I'd been, at his unconscious behest, tending his anger all my conscious life, all while he was protecting me from feeling any of my own. It was a double bind, that psychological reality I'd find out about decades later that creates craziness, and which includes, as one of its many symptoms, outbursts of anger.

I had no language then, for this understanding now. But of course, a rock doesn't know when it's time to cleave itself from itself. And although I'm not my Dad, our DNA speaks otherwise, as would any selfie with us side by side. We look the same, we process much of the world in exactly the same way. And my wife has said more times than I can count that I behave just like him, especially when it comes to interpreting the relational fireworks that can go off in a living room or over a dinner conversation.

One can't become the thing one is attached to without finally detaching from it. And it makes sad, crazy sense that Dad, who had no Dad to release himself from, wouldn't know how much I needed to be able to do that myself, with him. It makes sense that he would, quite naturally, hold on all the more tightly to something he never had in the first place, creating a vacuum. And seeing as nature abhors a vacuum, and hatred and anger are bedfellows, our relationship revolved, like a Colt .45, around anger.

That is, until something changed. I'm still not sure what that something is. But Dad greets me at the door now, when I come to see him.

Joylyn Chai's writing has appeared in *The Fiddlehead, The Ex-Puritan, Ricepaper, The Cincinnati Review*, and elsewhere. Her essays have been nominated for a Pushcart Prize and selected as notable for The Best American Essays 2024. Joylyn is Chinese-Jamaican Canadian and teaches adult learners and newcomers on the traditional territories of Tkaronto/Toronto.

She Should Be Released

There is nothing to look forward to except for rearranging the furniture so she can roll up the area rugs to take to the cleaners. The worn wool smells like a wet dog. The grit left on the empty wooden floor is flecked with sparkles, like mica, creating little rock constellations. Decorations and celebrations have shed their sheen. She's sweeping up sand, dust, skin, and glitter; her happiest moments reduced to dry dirt. If she took the time to decipher the signs, the glitter would reveal her fortune. But with the speed of her broom and the urgency to get the surface mopped, she doesn't dare stop to see what fate lies ahead.

The task is more important than if her unhappiness lived forever.

Her husband's prescription is neatly worded in simple and direct language: *be kind.* Kindness is the antidote for her complicated aggression. Today, her kindness has crawled under the bed and is hiding. Also today, the news reported that two people, a boy of twelve and a man of twenty, went on a violent spree in the city, attacking vagrants and the homeless. They were armed with a hammer. Sometimes she wonders what force she could yield with the claw of a heavy hammer and the swell of her right hand in anger. She has never trusted her physical strength to match the violence of her thoughts.

Of course, he prefers her cheerful, but not joyous. Excitability in women is generally frowned upon. Playfulness is superfluous. Controlled charm is ideal. So then. How should she share her thoughts about the quotidian events of her day? He says, "You don't have any trouble talking. You have so many words." He's forever counting the words, which means nothing can ever be shared. She says, "We've evolved so our arms can swing out in a wide arc. We can lock eyes with someone we trust and yell, 'Catch!'" He looks at her momentarily, like a passenger peering out the window of a bus in rush hour. His mind belongs to a stranger. He easily moves away from her, as if she's never said a word to him before.

When she was pregnant, she would wake at night, her dark fatigue swirling around her, a slow-moving mist from a dream. She often thought of Jacques-Louis David's painting, *The Death of Marat.* Jean-Paul Marat's skin condition and opinions required attention while soaking in a bathtub. In death, with his head wrapped in a towel, he is beautiful; his politics seem irrelevant, as does his martyrdom. One night, she wrote furiously about a feminist-guerrilla uprising with their leader murdered, the same as Marat, in a tub. The memory of her midnight loneliness holds a strange comfort. Nothing in her daytime relationship—in her marriage—can be resolved so easily as death.

She told her husband he's like a kite. He's sailing upon invisible ridges carved by the blowing air. The red kite and tail jerk and twirl with unexpected speed. She imagines the kite with arms. Thin limbs opening, closing, and twisting, able to express lyrical movement, but not the song of anyone's soul. She let go of the kite, the silk string limp, dangling and ugly, unable to match the grace of the crimson tail dancing in the wind.

Christine Vartoughian is an award-winning, Armenian-American writer and film director. Her work has shown at Lincoln Center, the Museum of the Moving Image (MoMI), and her feature film, *Living with the Dead: A Love Story*, is available on AppleTV and Amazon Prime. Her short fiction has been published in *Parley, The Bookends Review, Rock Salt Journal, Audience Askew* literary magazine and others. Her book of stories, *The Only Way Out Is Through the Window*, was published in July 2025 by Rebel Satori Press.

Retreat the Queen

A rush of blood to my head as I think of his skin. I want to split it open. I want her skin, too. I want to slip it on, slide inside, and hear him whisper his chalkboard love poems to me in the middle of the night. I want to be her and breathe her and breed her, all at once. I want to be the one he wants.

It's my desire to be desired that will kill me.

I check over my shoulder to make sure no one can hear. Even though these thoughts are only in my head, they are so strong, it feels like I am screaming them out loud. I'm back in his bar after a two-week hiatus. Neither of us mention the last time I saw him.

Did he see me watching him? With her?

We laugh and joke, and he gives me free drinks. We play chess. I stare at his face as he stares at the board, and find it so much more interesting than any game. I play by my own rules, moving the pieces based on silly ideas I make up in the moment, like how I can only play pieces that are shorter than the last one he moved, or pieces that create a hidden pattern only I can see. I make shapes across the board as he captures my players; their loss doesn't matter.

When the game is over, I finish the last sips of my drink and decide it's time for me to go, to quit while I'm ahead, while he's smiling at me. The way he looks at me as he hugs me goodbye makes me hope that the girl I saw him kissing last time I walked by is out of the picture, erased from the pattern. When I'm halfway down the block, I turn and see him watching me, still smiling. I smile back.

Every time I leave him, it's with regret. It's the only way I can go. I wait, and wait, and wait, and let the time pass until it's made something of itself, something meaty, and then, after time has grown stale and brittle, that's when I choose my exit.

On my way home, I wonder if I'm in love with him. I've been dreaming about him, but I dream about a lot of things, and I'm old enough to know that dreams don't always mean anything or always steer me straight. Dreams are only just that— dreams. Dreams full of nothing. Dreams made to trick me, to make me go around and around and around. Dreams with easy smiles that say nothing about where they come from or what they represent.

Before I know it, I'm on my street, walking towards my building, shrouded in the falling leaves of dying trees below stars of a sad night. I am walking straight ahead, destined for my destination, the same one every time. I have left him far behind. Choosing to go when I could have stayed, choosing solitude when I could be in his company.

I chose to quit. I choose this path over and over. I see myself walking down it without any courage, without even a thought of turning back.

Him smiling at me...

I want to exist in that space of time forever.

Like what I had failed to do in my dreams when I had spilled the bloody mess and unleashed evil everywhere. My own sopping wet Pandora's jar. Every smile I've ever been given, I keep stored away, archived and preserved like pickles or strawberry jam, like no-longer-living sea creatures washed up on shore. Like the queen in her final moments, trying to save herself, retreating and alone.

Poems

and Prose

K.R. Morrison is a San Francisco poet who splits her time between the Bay Area and Southern California. She is a three-time Pushcart Nominee, and her first collection of poems, *Cauldrons*, was published in July 2021 by Paper Press Books. Morrison is also a drummer, an online writing workshop teacher, a natal chart intuitive interpreter, and a tarot reader.

Here & Now

my breath is a blessing, loss

that departs   every exhale, possibility

held by hope   i inhale

i am an ocean

of rebirths, murder story

in the reefs of me

who am i radically unbecoming?

i am made of moon scars & stories

some i carry are mine

i incant them

every morning, an overthrow

every night, a reckoning

Night Mother escorts me
in our wane she guides me
back to loss stuffed with fire

My aunt. She says
god stores every tear
i've cried in a bottle*

that he scribes each one of them
down in scripture, that's one hell
of a coin collection.

All points of the pentacle are sacred.

in a world that swears on everything
it is not safe to be myself
let the wound breathe in witness

who i was to stay safe,

pirate girl conditioned

to be seen & not heard

who i actually am

a pandora's box of feral graves

show me how to use this darkness

feed the right wolf, momma

move the world

with grief

moonlight

in my lungs –

* Psalm 56 V. 8

Lacuna

i become the vessel pour memory into the ocean
empty you & me into sacred pause
where bullets & battle axes lose their voices

i inhale silence   souls rest in stars
in stillness what's quiet screams who we are
becoming who we have been retreats, exhausted

into caskets. Silence is armed
strapped in portals i am not afraid of what's soundless
but what arrives & leaves in the shouting

in the violence into a mirror we tumble, steaming
of us   we are raw & exhausted running
away from ourselves   while we fight brave

admirable battles for better worlds
we've yet to uncover within ourselves.

the gift is in the wound.

into mouths of snakes shedding
searching for moondaughter skin
joy hides a landmine, too many stories

bleed out
into graveyards haunted
by lost war horses

follow the fire craving a torch
from ash hear ghosts
of every woman she became

to mother the eras
of girls inside her, searching
for a womb

the gift is in the wound.

in the unbecoming
of memory's mourning breath
cremate guardian angels

armed with ten swords
hunting for sore backs burdened
by evil eyes. in the bones

of every soul journey
are teams of demons cursed
with childhoods and a conscience

the gift is in the wound.

in the shedding she returns
to the dark, where dawn pours
nectarine gold onto her

outgrown ribcaves. in the wound
she returns to herself
on her shoulder a sea hawk

in her fist
a sickle for reaping
star harvests.

Poet Prayer

Wear the words.
Climb inside the consonants

like a child between parents.
When those who ghost evoke night

terrors, light a match. Call on fire
to release their silence

For all those word abusers
hide clown traps. On a new moon

plant your wounded catch
beneath sapphire fields

of wildflowers, beneath what's green
set them free. Invoke water

gods to wash their dirty
lips, cleanse damage

from toxic tongues who infect
words, so they infect us.

To love illiterates
stop writing.

Love in MexicoWhen he speaks

Diego murals

summon an altar of lips

she basements inside bruised ears

In her heart's attic

she listens and collects

fresh thoughts falling, searing

cobwebs off Trotsky red

Love graffiti's rawboned eyes

irises green dismiss what's grey

her naked mind imbrued

moon blue, electrified.

previously published in Switchback a USF Literary Magazine, 2016.

Emma Kennedy. is a teacher studying for a Master's Degree, and loves writing poems.

Friends for Life's Long Path

New friends

and new laughs.

New voices

and held hands.

They can make a big difference to how you feel.

When life gets you down

and it feels like all is lost,

those new friends

and new laughs

and held hands

can really save the day.

It can be hard

to make new friends

and you have to be really careful

with who you can trust.

But overtime

you learn,;

which ones were the best

new friends for you

and who will be joining you

along life's long path.

I Chose The Water

Confusion and pain are always the strongest

currents inside.

Suddenly coming back; far too familiar,

On the shore/in deep,

It's never felt safe to me: it's cold.

I'll drown in it.

But I was on the sand

when the lightening started.

And it still hurts, even now.

I still think of you; despite everything....

That's why I always go the long way round, by myself;

but yesterday I took the salt path

and walked alone, slowly home

with my feet in the sea.

I binned my trainers afterward

but—

I chose the water on the day that I was born.
Being strong and able; chubby and long.
Head first and arms first: I chose the water.
Floating, thrusting, swimming,
moving forward, keeping going...

And where there's pain,
I'll always choose the water
And where there's no pain,
I'll always choose the water.
I think the children I have taught
chose the water as well.
And my baby, at three weeks, laughed at the cold
and laughed at the water.

The Deer in Burghley Park

To one especially, I got close.
Whilst to most,
there's too much fear;
before running to safety elsewhere.

It was unsafe, gazing.
I took a million pictures of The Stag
and zoomed in on his coat:
stunning. Against the Earth and sky.

I bought a pot of tea at The Orangery
and took the last train home.
Alone. As always these days.

Except, memories are like photographs
and he is still there, looking back.
I've realised I had forgotten

how wild he was.

Free at last.

How wild he was.

I cropped the photos of the stag.

Cool and calm. Relaxed.

I airbrushed many of myself.

I'm not like him.

My hair has grown dark at the roots again.

It's long and maybe wild.

Sometimes I kid myself

and I believe

I'm free at last as well.

Autumn Williams is the author of two poetry books: her chapbook *Waves*, and her number one bestselling collection *Clouds on the Ground*. Her poems have been featured in *Poetic Reveries Magazine*, the *Roots and Ruins* anthology (Arcana Poetry Press), and multiple other publications. She also earned a finalist spot in *The Wishing Shelf Book Awards*. Her work is influenced by the chronic illness she has, Myalgic Encephalomyelitis, but is written to be universal. Williams lives in Texas with her husband and their children.

Forgetting

There is a road of forgetting
where you sit and watch shadows.
The car you ride in
is empty except for you—
or maybe
a ghost drives it.
There are no cities, or tiny towns—
only hills and too many stars.
This highway removes pain,
and leaves a hollow fear
of something you can't remember.

Waiting Time

There is no chair or bookshelf.
The window isn't unlatched.
A box in the corner remains unopened—
its tape fused into the cardboard.
Nothing has happened
inside this room
in all of its
waiting
time.

Held

The world is paused perfectly

with your arm around my shoulders.

I listen to the sound of your steady breathing,

and the moment becomes a held,

unshattered

memory.

Close

They told me not to walk that way,

so I didn't,

but I got as close to the edge as I could,

to look at the view of miles

cut off from the world with an invisible fence.

Some Other Version of Earth

Just above the black trees'
silhouette,
the sky is the palest shade of yellow.

As I stare I can tell
it's opened a portal
to some other version of earth
that never existed.

If I could climb to the top
of the trees, I would let go,
and fly right into it.

Patrick Trombly returned to writing poetry for publication in 2025, after a 35-year hiatus. He writes in a variety of formats including sonnets, villanelles, haiku, haibun and free verse. His poems explore the relationships among humans, nature, time, the afterlife and the divine. His poems have been published or accepted for publication in the *Dewdrop, Loch Raven Review, Beyond Words, Wingless Dreamer, Hemlock Journal,*

and the Quillkeepers Press sonnet anthology. Patrick lives in NYC with his partner, his two stepdaughters, and two cats. 'Red Tail' is a modified haibun in which the prose section is broken into layers, like the cliffs referenced therein, and the haiku is presented floating across the page, like the clouds that are referenced throughout the poem. It is about fate and the impersonal, uncaring forces of the universe that come together to decide our fates, over minutes, hours, or millions of years. And it is about the quiet moment in which we take that all in, before acting. It is a coiled spring.

Red Tail

In the distance, pink cliffs form a border running the width of the horizon. It is a glowing pink, hot, reflecting sunlight bleeding through the clouds behind me. The rain that fell this morning has stopped for the day. I know this from the color of the cliffs before I know it from the dryness reclaiming its chokehold on the air.

The cliffs have layers. Green lines fill the crevices between the layers, like mortar.

The green lines give way to green swatches and then a green carpet—a light green carpet darkening and deepening, becoming shag as it gently rolls downgrade toward me. The carpet eventually gives way to discernible junipers holding gray-blue berries.

Some of the water from the morning shower will disappear into the dryness and rejoin the clouds. The rest will sink into the sand accumulating from the gradually collapsing dune behind me. I had to shimmy down the dune to reach the rock ridge on which I stand.

The dune and ridge were once seabed. The sea is now five hundred miles away.

I had knelt to take a photograph of a waterlogged cactus with its yellow flowers reopening.

I stood back up, and I looked out across the wash that has carried the runoff from the red ridge, and then past the wash, a field of sparse sage, and then the junipers, fifty yards away.

I stand still on the ridge, silently surveying this rough country. The ridge is redder than the cliffs. Most of the terrain I have hiked through is red like that. Is it Heaven, as they call it? Yes, in a way, but it is not Eden. I look down, and I notice a gray hare. I nod, to acknowledge him. The hare stares up at me, breathing between heartbeats that I can see pulsing beneath his coarse coat: inhale – twenty beats – exhale.

He stands like a statue behind a boulder next to a puddle in a dip that the wind scooped out of a slab that lies flat on the ridge. The carving out probably happened fifty, perhaps a hundred, million years ago. The puddle is clear and unreflective in its red stone basin. The hare must have come out from under the junipers to drink from the puddle. Neither of us moves or makes a sound. Yet I know what he is thinking.

The rain will not return to wet feathers and interfere with flight. The sky will not go dark for five hours. But it will not be clear. He must run. He must run now. He must run blind.

vote to drop water

shifting consensus of clouds

vote to snuff shadows

Ursula McCabe lives in Oregon, USA. She likes forests, oceans, ospreys, dogs, and thrift shops. The order changes like the weather. She has a few things published, but not many, so she continues to lick the stamps.

nod to spring

buds are shy
it begins
tender forest unfurls

I search in the fronds of ferns
behind a winter felled fallen tree
whose bark-like flesh
opens to the sky
a supplication of sorts

finally the wooded floor
offers up
the nodding white trillium—
sage green veins spider thin
adorn each
milky white petal
a beacon of early spring

lonely are the first ones—
who come from dark earth

such delicate blooms

Your Voice

Grab the shape
that runs by quickly
a shadow with sound
whoosh
stomach clenches, you hear
something sigh, a thin wail,
it might have been your own voice.

Let us find our small places—
sing to the wind,
skin to skin, dirt to dirt,
tree to tree— succumb.

Be the live beat of pulsing blood,
swim upstream, spawn with salmon,
stretch your hook nose
open up gills, breathe.

Let common things come alive,

catch your footing.

Let language be salve—

coo like a dove, but be heard,

even if it comes out as a whisper,

our throats will clear.

The Errant Scrap

It was a college town, at the end of term time,
us high school girls
mingled with the college crowd
and got invited to a party.

Country Joe and the Fish played full blast.
Next up, *Jimmy Hendrix's* guitar
found me buried deep
in a dark red beard,
hands explored, we heavy necked till he
whispered with hot breath
I'm leaving town tonight, hitchhiking west.

He said he'd leave his signet ring and
a love note wrapped
in a blue bandanna, then bury it near
the water tower outside town.

The next few days, I spent digging
under the army green tower,
its giant green legs shaded me from June sun.
I never found my pouch of treasure.

Here I am, a lifetime has passed —
I can't remember his name or barely
what he looked like, but I hold that
musky memory somewhere in my skin.

Maybe just today, some 50-plus years later
a long-tailed magpie digs up
that tattered piece of paper,
the tuxedo-colored bird drops the
crumpled ball onto
a random yard. A young woman walks out,
picks up the errant scrap,
uses the flat of her hand
to straighten it out on her thigh.

She reads the paper, the scribbles are faint
with age, but still —moments later
her cheeks flush with pleasure.

Streak of Indigo

The past two weeks of rain
have freshened the farmland trail,
confused the grass,
which should be marching
to autumn's golden drummer.
Oak trees begin tossing rusty leaves,
but grass is having a sap green day.

An indigo blue streak
flashes eyebrow marks of white,
scrub jay
chats away,
leading me down her trail,
reminding me in bird speak—
that I'm only visiting.

Sun pushes me on,
a gentle hand on my back.

I've almost completed my circle
when finally I hear what I came for,
their gurgles, liquid bird-purrs
will keep me enchanted
throughout the long winter.

A throng of flapping wings
flies overhead,
whispered strength from feathers and chest—
the sandhill cranes are back.

January

Winter is the hardest season—
she knew this as she bundled up
went outside, plucked
the tiny bird off the dead clematis bush
then wrapped its iridescent green feathers
carefully in her warm hands
took it in the house
to defrost.

Over her shoulder, he says
the hummingbird is dead
but still—
together they took turns touching drops of sugar
to the needle-like beak
hoping for a revival
a catch of breath
watching for the pinhead-sized eyes to
flit open.

Then the couple would hug each other for what
felt like forever
which they did
even though the smallest flutter
never came to the small creature
on its blue washcloth bed.

Eleonora Baggio Compagnucci is a poet and independent researcher, obtained a master's degree in Architecture from the Politecnico di Milano in 2010, and works full-time in corporate. In July 2024, she founded the Collettivo Sincronie for travelling poetry alongside her fellow poets Anna Rita Germinario, Giulia Castelli, Sabrina Tolve. She lives in San Benedetto del Tronto where she writes by the Adriatic Sea. Some of her poems have been published in Italian blogs, newspapers and anthologies. @trottolaele (on Instagram)

Untitled

No one is willing to explain
how to switch off all the stars in the sky
how to reassemble crystal shards
without knowing what is the original item.

Bleak echoes glare
the hand clings
the cloth breaks
you feel like a foreigner
on earth
under the skin.

Untitled

If you scrape off the silver film from a mirror
and then overturn it,
you will see a turmoil of words—
they push to get out

the ardour and the stitches
keeping together the body—
they tug from the inside out

the siege of life and its empty chair
taken away

Ophelia is here
Stripped —but still alive.

Untitled

It is but a desire

to sleep

abandon the body, the watch over borders

every fiber fray in the breath

peace to you, peace to your sleep

sheep to count in heaven and on earth

outlines of blue-tinged mountains,

cold embers at dawn

to dream —persistently

to make it a shield

upon awakening.

Untitled

I wait on the balcony the time when
the sky fades and the night rests
between the dust of exhausted sparks and
the gold
of palm trees

the tide rises, embroidering foam laces

when it looks up to me I bleed again
to the rythm of the wave that retreats from the
shore
and repeats *I'll come back.*

Untitled

People passing by

they know nothing about my struggles

and I know nothing about their lives

solitudes, isolation and the quest

for love

the battle for being seen

in full light:

I hope I could be the switch

to turn the light on.

Deborah R. Majors has had poems and short stories published in *Blackwater Review; The Dead Mule School of Southern Literature; Deep South Magazine, Emerald Coast Review, Last Syllable,* among many others. Living the country life in Northwest Florida's Panhandle, and having dabbled in goat and chicken raising in the past, homeschooling, and collecting all things "bees," she now finds time to write between her responsibilities as Sr. Pastor of a non-denominational church, being a wife, mother of two grown sons, a mother-in-law, and Aunt Bee to many great-nieces-and-nephews. She enjoys swimming and exercising in her pool, family gatherings, and is a grateful cancer survivor who finds pleasure and beauty in simply waking up every morning—even if she finds a new wrinkle! She's just so happy to be alive!

Wal-Mart Bags

I saw,
    pushed by a semi's draft,
    Florida's snow
    float from heaven
    to Pine
    to grass
    then tumbleweed
    along the right of way
    journeying to somewhere else—
    anywhere else—
    until captured by thorny-fingered vines
    or pinecones
    or barbed wire
    or a smirking sign claiming
    a *$500.00 fine* before saluting
    every passerby
    along the two-laned state highway,
    man's territory, scented and marked
    with musky-yellow double stripes.

I saw
    a crow enter a handle-lipped
    plastic-white womb
    then was birthed
    with a cupcake creamed beak,
    a Hostess gift.

I saw,
    tied with bungee cords
    and pink ribbon to a
    Rural Route mailbox,
    poor man's balloons
    stuffed with pine straw and oak leaves

flagging the party's location.

I saw,
on the Mid-Bay Bridge,
wind-filled blindness dive-bomb
a teenage Yamaha rider.

I saw
crunchy wads
recycled at the health food store
by a skinny old hippie—
"Turn them inside out at least;
hide the name that's not yours."

"Can't do that," he whispered,
de-wrinkling
ink with colloidal silver,
goat's milk soap, and Vitamin C,
"Best to show the nature of the beast."

---

previously published in:Blackwater Review: A Journal of Literature and Art, Spring 2007 Deep South Magazine 2013

live dangerously

today:

let the toilet paper roll
flow under instead of over

don't make the bed

go the speed limit

put a period after your signature

check email
once

don't dot your i's

drink straight
from the milk carton

squeeze out the teabag with 2 spoons
instead of that stringed paper tag

drive a different route to work

without talking
look straight into my eyes

one full minute

previously published in: Blackwater Review: A Journal of Literature and Art, Spring 2013

Weigh One's Words

How many stones does an insult weigh?
How many
ounces a compliment? Why does grief
heap pressing
pounds, bending bleak heads so low,
but joy lades only
by the mere milligram, written in vanishing
ink? Mmm. This, I think,
is how an epiphany
feels: free, warm and precise,
no showy thunderclaps,
no robed choir, just a mulish resolve destiny
delivers for our good.
For writing this poem enwraps
vivid awareness that only I can assign
weight to words—only I fix burden, benefit,
or ballast to words that wing my way—I align
my emotions and draft their sway to elicit
the mass displayed by the scale. Epiphany or
no, *I'll* peg all words, for words, I cannot ignore.

Veronica Tucker is an emergency medicine and addiction medicine physician, mother of three, and lifelong New Englander. Her poetry explores the intersections of medicine, motherhood, memory, and being human. Her work appears in *One Art, Eunoia Review, Berlin Literary Review,* and in *The Book of Jobs* anthology. She released a chapbook collection, The House as Witness (Quillkeepers Press, 2026). Veronica shares more at veronicatuckerwrites.com and on Instagram @veronicatuckerwrites.

The Silence That Holds

The room does not argue with itself.
It waits,
the window open just enough
to let in a breeze carrying
yesterday's rain.

I stand with a glass of water,
listening to the pipes
shift in the walls,
to the faint click
of cooling metal.

Every silence has a memory inside it.
The refrigerator hum recalls
nights I stayed awake on purpose,
counting heartbeats against the dark.
The floor remembers
every step I took
when I thought no one was listening.

I used to think change arrived
with sirens,
with declarations,
with a certainty that broke doors open.

Now I know it comes
as softly as breath.
It waits in the pause
before I speak,
in the hesitation that teaches me
the value of restraint.

Here, in stillness,
a new kind of courage grows,
quiet but insistent,
a rebellion of not rushing,
not filling,
not apologizing,
simply letting the silence
speak for itself.

Cup on the Counter

The mug waits,
a thin rim of tea cooling
to the color of late afternoon.

No one has claimed it yet.
The house holds the cup
like a secret,
its handle turned slightly
toward the sink.

I could empty it.
I could wash it clean
and place it back in the cupboard
with the rest,
lined like soldiers
behind a wooden door.

Instead, I leave it,
half-filled,

a witness to the fact
that nothing is ever completed
all at once.

A cup abandoned
reminds me of the time
I held my child too tightly,
afraid she would slip
from the circle of my arms.
It reminds me
of the unfinished sentence
my patient never finished
before the monitor flattened.

It is rebellion enough
to let what is incomplete remain.
A cup, a story, a life paused mid-breath.
Even the smallest vessel
can carry what spills over,
reminder, warning, prayer.

Soft Armor

The blanket at the edge of the couch
remembers the weight of a child.
I fold it slowly,
though I know it will not stay folded.

There is defiance in the repetition.
Every crease is a quiet oath
to keep making order
even when the world
unravels.

I think of patients
wrapping themselves
in the thin warmth of hospital sheets,
the way they cling to fabric
as though it could carry them
through withdrawal, through pain,

through the long nights
when even their own skin
feels borrowed.
The blanket here carries
softer rebellions:
the nap abandoned,
the dream interrupted,
the small body
choosing sleep over struggle.
I lift it to my chest,
the scent of detergent and skin
rising like incense.
I refold it knowing
it will come undone again,
its loosening not a failure,
but proof
that someone has been held.

Quiet Hours

The clock does not rush me.
Its hands move,
but with the patience of an old friend
crossing the street,
waving in no hurry to arrive.

I write a list
I may never finish.
The paper curls slightly
beneath my palm,
as though it already knows
my failures and forgives them.

Outside,
pine needles bend
under invisible wind,
a chorus of quiet percussion
I am not required to conduct.

Inside,
the hum of the heater

fills the spaces between thoughts.
I do not silence it.
I let its drone braid itself
into my pulse.

We are trained to measure hours
by productivity,
by what can be crossed off.
But rebellion is slower,
less visible.

It is choosing to pause
in the middle of a list.
It is letting the kettle whistle
without leaping to answer.
It is the quiet defiance
of letting time loosen its grip,
becoming water
that carries me,
with no demand
I control the current.

Breath Between Words

You speak,

then stop,

and in the air

between your sentence and mine

a truth gathers weight.

We are taught to patch silence

like a leaking roof,

to fill it quickly

before the rain comes in.

But tonight I let the pause widen.

I let it stretch long enough

to feel the shape of it.

It is not absence.

It is not threat.

It is the body's reminder

that breath comes first,

that every word is born
from what we do not say.

I think of the patient
who asked me if anyone
would listen if he stopped talking.
I told him silence
has its own grammar,
its own rebellion.

Here, between us,
I practice leaving space open.
I allow the unsaid
to be an answer.

Sometimes the boldest act
is not explanation
but restraint,
a refusal to break the weight
of what lingers.

Michele Harvey's poems have appeared in several literary journals including: *Progenitor, Copper Nickel*, and *The Litchfield Review*. Her sonnet, "Dinosaur Ridge," was chosen as the focal point for a permanent art in public places display at the Jefferson County Government Center railway station in Golden, Colorado. She is the author of the self-published poetry collection, *Poetry for Living an Inspired Life*.

Surrender

I close my eyes to inhale
the sleepy rhythm of the rain
to feel it empty me of pleasure,
as it empties me of pain.
Warmed beyond the waters
as they wash away time,
I bear witness to the rainbow:
my trappings left behind.

previously published in Poetry for Living an Inspired Life (self-published, 2013)

Remembering

My truth dwells within the coolness
of quiet spaces.
Today, while I was sitting, eyes closed, it arrived
in the four-syllable shrill of a multi-colored bird,
just beyond my vision.
I followed its repetition until a familiar voice
embraced me in the tingling light,
and I knew that I know.
It is me I must follow.

previously published in Poetry for Living an Inspired Life (self-published, 2013)

Charlene Stegman Moskal is a Teaching Artist for SPRAT Interdisciplinary Arts Program and the Las Vegas Poetry Promise Organization. She is published in numerous anthologies, print and online magazines including: *TAB Journal; Calyx, Humana Obscura,* and *Mslexia.* Her chapbooks are *One Bare Foot,* (Zeitgeist Press), Leavings from My Table, (Finishing Line Press), Woman Who Dyes

Her Hair (Kelsay Books) and a full length poetry collection Running the Gamut (Zeitgeist Press).

Warnings

So, there's this place we stopped to grieve.
It wasn't in our plans, but we stopped anyway
less than forty miles from home
along the road through the Sunrise Mountains
on the way to the Valley of Fire;

an oasis with palms and warm flowing water
gurgling as if the rocks were instructed
to make comfort sounds.
But there were danger signs, warnings
to not bathe or even touch the water; strange,

because of the life it gave on its periphery,
just like you, against whom I was told
to be cautious. They weren't all wrong
and I was never more forgiving
or more in love when I dove in all the way,

over my head, rose to your surface

without ever opening my eyes

until at the end I peeked; by then it was too late,

the tides of you awoke the rhythms of me

and I embraced my choice with all I could offer.

Trust is the First Word

Hold my secrets in the palm of your hand,
treat them with care;
loosely close your fingers around them
as you would a fledgling bird found outside its nest,

as you would hold a dandelion's gray head
for just a moment, then send the remnants
of what was once golden aloft
with each tiny seed, its own promise.

Bring your hand to your ear,
wait until whispers of my past
tell stories of what I think was true,
swirl soft as new snow.

Listen for all the *I love you's*

said with hope, and those said
without expectation of response
but given anyhow.

I have chosen to put my closeted truths
where caresses and slaps live side by side,
offer them to you without reserve;
trust is the first word you will hear.

If I have revealed too much
don't open your hand or turn it face down
when your palm grows heavy—
there is nothing I expect you to say.

After Thirty Years

She comes into the room like fog;
covers pieces of their leftover lives
with a cloak made of damp air.

Or perhaps not fog but sea foam; deceptive
as if solid, able to be held in your hand,
the lace doily of a grandmothers' legacy.

She is silent— inhales memories from before;
lavender perhaps and his patchouli,
the scent of cigarettes and sex sweat.

She wears determination like a silk scarf,
wrapped securely, protective,
across her shoulders.

She speaks with a voice nuanced as fog,
delicate as sea foam, redolent as morning after's,
strong, resilient as silk;

Watch where I go from here!

Erick Phillips Garske is a poet, spoken word artist, father, and author of the full-length poetry collection, Words Alone. He is a Pushcart Prize nominee. He lives in Southern California with a young dog, a Cavalier, near his two adult sons.

Mission Bells

just as music
is space
between
notes

just as my longing
is time
between
your glances

just as yearning
is absence
between
your embrace

mission bells
toll
until
your return

previously published Festival of Poetry, July 2025

Woodwind

The breeze brushes through

fragrant autumn eucalyptus leaves.

Leaves slowly rustle,

pater, and rise

to a crescendo

like a woodwind instrument

improvising,

inspired

by the wonder that abounds.

Definitions

You will not let definitions define you.
If you were to be used in a sentence,
you would begin with a wordless longing
that would transcend language and speech

in the way that wind speaks to the waves,
the way the tide enunciates with lips
against a shoreline,
the way the breeze whispers into the ears of corn
telling them to dance naked in a summer field
on the graves of their ancestors.

previously published Art Inscribed, August 2025

Pamela Mathison-Levitt is a disabled writer and homeschooling mom. Mathison-Levitt's work has appeared in *WWPH Writes*, *Mid-Atlantic Review*, *Exposed Brick Literary Magazine*, *Pen in Hand*, *Emerald Coast Review*, *Literary Mama's* blog and other publications. You can find her work on Facebook at Lines and Branches or on Instagram @pmmlevitt.

One Among Many

"Love means to learn to look at yourself/The way one looks at distant things/For you are only one thing among many."
—Czeslaw Milosz

When I pray for the relief of all suffering,
I feel the pangs of a mother's empty stomach.
I look through a morgue window,
and listen to the pulse of a heart rate monitor.

When I pray for the relief of all suffering,
I feel the phantom pain of lost limbs;
I look through an empty bottle,
and listen to tears falling on a pillow.

When I pray for relief,
I feel the hard comfort of a prayer bead
rolling between my fingers.
I look over a still lake in the morning
and listen to the sound of the owl at dusk
as it calls back an answer.

Unspoken

The days never written about
still leave marks,

streaks on hair,

lines under eyes
and around mouths,

tracks on the Earth,

particles dispersed
by the smallest breath,

grooves worn on matter,

strokes on skin and hair,
shifting dust to the ground

where it forms the loam
and growth can begin.

Daniel Conigliaro is a middle school Social Studies and Religion teacher in Jacksonville, FL. He attended the University of Florida, where he received a Bachelor's in History and Classical Studies and a Master's in History. Through poetry, he seeks to discover meaning in the mundane and to understand the deepest parts of the human experience.

My Shame Has Reared Its Ugly Head Before

My shame has reared its ugly head before.
He knows my deepest thoughts and where I live.
He makes his presence felt right to my core
and robs my soul of all I have to give.
He haunts my dreams and makes my night as day
and snatches rest right out from my weak grasp.
He sends me down a tailspin of dismay
into his wretched arms and fear-gripped clasp.
I feel the hangman's noose around my neck.
His twisted rope digs deep into my veins,
cuts sinews, flesh, but keeps his force in check
and lets me live to prove he holds the reins—
the reins *I* gave him, when my heart was fair.
The noose was mine, 'twas I who put it there.

Sitting on the beach on a foggy afternoon

The fog consumes me, sucks me into its pull,
wraps me tight around like a wet, used towel.
White caps surge and crest,
cascading down like dominoes,
blankets of grey on grey stacked
above the sheets of waves
that drown out thoughts with *shushing* sounds,
my mind silent as a funeral parlor.
I hear a seagull sing a dirge
for a lost companion.
He flies into view for a moment, then disappears
in the cloudy, winter day. I see people now
materialize like phantoms
build bodies out of thin air; their
corporeal forms pass before me,
smile, wave, nod,

then fade back into

wispy, airy mist

before vanishing from sight

(he once vanished too

in a box underground

and so did she and she).

The sea grows stronger now.

Memories flood my brain and pull me under.

The air is dense and matted.

It wants to steal my form. I won't let it—

not today, anyway—there are still too many

errands to run before going home.

K.L. Johnston is an award-winning author, photographer, and poet best known for works centered on spiritual experience, nature, and trauma survival. Author of three books of poetry, *In Every Season*, *The Nature of These Gifts*, and *Grace Period*, her poetry can be found in literary magazines and anthologies both in print and online. A retired antiques and art dealer, she currently lives near the Savannah River. You can find out more at www.Facebook.com/Kathleen-Johnston or visit her online gallery at 1-kathleen-johnston.pixels.com.

for P.M.

I want to thank you

for that morning in the parking lot

when the light

was pouring from the east

and cheerful, you shushed us,

our group chattering like starlings,

you, pointing skyward

into the morning

as we all stood awed

watching the flight

of that one whimbrel

circling, gliding, singing,

flying out of the sun.

previously published in Hot Poet Equinox. 22 September 2024

On Jarvis Creek

The wood stork landed in a whoosh
and a flurry, shoulders broad
as a stevedore, wrinkled bald head,
bright eyes staring. Wings white as angels
visiting in stained glass morning light.

Solemn, he started the dance, forward
three steps, half turn wing-shimmy three steps
back, beak raised, then head thrust down, step
step, step, shimmy turn, furl wings.
Offshore in deep water, unblinking

the alligator watched, a dreadnought
at rest. No one else was there
to see but me on my morning
walk with the sun as the stork danced,
fluffed his ruff of down, shaking

his tail feathers, maybe in practice
for courtship. Maybe a dance of defiance,
a wing fingered gesture to all alligators.
Maybe dancing in that sheer joy
of being alive and able to fly away.

previously published in Midsummer Dream House Summer's Mixtape. 25 August 2025

September's High Places

City eyes don't see far well.

On the brow of the yellow hill, my lover

held me tight until I saw the doe

She caught our smell and fled,

a white star falling.

previously published in Kudzu No.3, Nov-Dec 1977

Carol Lynne Knight is co-director of Anhinga Press. Since 1992, she has edited and designed more than 150 literary publications for the press, including books by Diane Wakoski and Naomi Shihab Nye. She is the author of three books of poetry, *A Fretted Terrain, Like Mars* (Apalachee Press, 2020), *Quantum Entanglement* (Apalachee Press, 2010), and *If I Go Missing* (Fernwood Press, 2022). Her poetry has appeared in *Another Chicago*

Magazine, Louisiana Literature, Tar River Review, Poetry Motel, Earth's Daughters, The Ledge, Slipstream, Broome Review, Comstock Review, Northwest Florida Review, Epicenter, Redactions, So to Speak, and others. In other lives, she has worked as an art teacher, potter, videographer, copywriter, and graphic designer. She lives in Tallahassee, Florida.

Here Is a Box of Endings

a tender place where fevers break
and colicky babies drift to sleep,
where roads are lost to the forest or even the sea,
where blossoms drop into late spring grass
and an afternoon rain moves on, leaving
the earth to steam and hiss,
where night ends and sunlight breathes
and yawns between the backyard trees,
where a sunset languishes over
the mall's vast parking lot
and streetlights blink on, buzz and
spark against a russet sky,
where what begins shall end
and then begin again.
how the movie and its flicker finishes
with credits rolling,
the thrall of story still binding us
until the lights come up,
when you read all night to finish a novel

then mourn the final chapter for a week,
how the last embrace seems much like the first,
how a kiss that means goodbye never feels final,
her last trip to the vet, her fragile body
cleaving to yours, the trembling.
here is the end of a nightmare
quelled by the approach of daylight.
a year in all its glory and fuss,
ends with midnight fireworks,
only to begin the count again in the morning.
adieu, we say at the end of our phone call,
then find one more thing to confide.
how many times to repeat amen at the end
of the song, the last note hovering over us —
imagining my last breath, all that ends with it,
and my suspicions about what shall then begin.

Steph Percival is an Atlantic Canadian writer, mom, and sheepadoodle walker. Her work has been featured in the 2025 Central Avenue Poetry Prize Anthology, *SAPP Zine*, and Swim Press, and she has work forthcoming in several anthologies. You can find her poetry online at @thismanywords on Instagram.

For An Afternoon, Pause and Imagine

We can make a sport of cloud watching;
of laying on our backs, tickled by a thousand
fingers of grass. Of letting our thoughts ebb
like the ocean as we look up at the broad,
nursery-hued sky. Nothing but your little
hands in mine, each year growing closer
to mine in size. Let us look up and watch
the clouds, these delectable whips
of buttercream frosting floating on by.
This is why we exist, our instincts to name
a winged thing out of wisps of cumulus
rival our instincts to survive. Let us lay here
in wholehearted bliss and see what gifts
visit us. Maybe we'll even spot a Pegasus.

I am learning

how to be still as a shoreline
how to let the waves crash upon me   and
even as I'm eroding, allow them
to cleanse me and retreat.

I am learning

how to ride the wave
of your heart's tempests
without my own becoming
shipwrecked.

I am learning

how to be the moon

how to be my own ebb and flow

how to ease my own rising tides.

You Could Make A Home Here

A susurration summons you, waves
you to walk into a meadow of wildflowers
and pussy willows. Step in to softly release
the tension in your heart.

Allow a moment for your eyes to adjust
to the saturation of purples, pinks, and yellows.
Only now are you aware how spectacularly
paint swatches fail to capture the infinite hues
of nature's colours.

Make a bed amidst the long, soft grasses
which sigh as you lay upon them. Let a giggle
lift off from your lips as bees nestled
in clover tickle your toes.

A ladybug circles your finger, as though
wedding you with an invisible ring, a promise
of eternity, while a kiss from a butterfly's
wings brushes your cheek.

Within the clearing, the sun's rays reach
to light you from without and within,
warming your skin.

At the meadow's edge, the trees stretch
up and out like great yawning beings,
obliging to provide you shelter, shade,
an umbrella when it rains.

You could make a home here. Make
merry with woodland kin, a modern-day
Snow White (minus her creepy brethren).

This poem is yours to dwell within.
You are welcome to visit often. Here,
you will always find this meadow.
You can always call it yours.

Liz Garden is a school principal by day, mom by night, and wanna-be writer in the random free moments in between. She is currently working on her MFA in Creative Nonfiction Writing from Bay Path University. Liz has served as an editorial advisor for *NAESP's Principal Magazine* for ten years and has written several education related articles and blog posts. She has contributed to two published books titled, *She Leads:The Woman's Guide to a Career in Educational Leadership* and *What Makes a Great Principal: The Five Pillars of Effective School Leadership.*

Mutation

Was it Grandma's vanity?
A childhood erased
No black and white history
All because of a minute mutation in the womb.
Half your face marked red,
Meant your early years were also marked
With surgeries, doctors, and meds.
She decided:
Radiate those confused capillaries away.

I close my eyes and see
The ridged landscape of your scarred skin
Just past your chin
Descending down,
Down your neck
Plateauing above the collarbone.
Your cosmetic cover up never fooled me,
I knew the secret your mother
Tried to burn,
The one you tried to conceal and not feel.

Was it that this outward mutation
Eradicated inward?
I envision
Something subtle
Something silently slipping
For years under your skin
Traveling within
Eventually coming to rest,
This time
in your breast.

Chop 'em both off!
You declared without hesitation.
I burned my bra a long time ago,
This body has no more
need for gestation.
Our femaleness is not defined
By my dense tissue or my mama's
Or her mama's.
You taught me that.
After the incisions,

After the drains,

After the implants and pain,

Reconstructed and scarred yet again,

This had to be the end

Of this mutation.

Was it autoimmune

Reasons that were the last straw?

The kid doctor in me,

The long-time live-forever-wisher in me

Thought your brain

Oughta be

Immune.

Mens sana in corpore sano

Those visible scars,

Reminders of battles won;

Surely *a healthy mind*

In a (mostly) *healthy body.*

But we couldn't see,

Wouldn't see,

That mutation,

Once charred, once chopped,
But never completely stopped,
Settled in
Embedded,
An invasive vine
Silently growing into your mind.
Surely this couldn't be
Because of
Grandma's vanity?

Carolyn Chilton Casas is a practicing Reiki Master and teacher who explores ways of healing in the articles she writes for energy and wellness magazines in several countries. Her poetry has appeared in journals such as *Braided Way*, *Grateful Living*, and *One Earth Sangha* and in anthologies including *The Wonder of Small Things: Poems of Peace and Renewal*, *Thin Spaces & Sacred Spaces*, and *Women in a Golden State*. More of Carolyn's work can be found on Instagram and Facebook, at www.carolynchiltoncasas.com, and in her newest collection of poetry, *Under the Same Sky*.

Astrophe

The feeling of being stuck on Earth, coined by John Koenig, "The Dictionary of Obscure Sorrows"

When the seer first finds her,
the little girl is pointing to a star,
making clear this was where
she'd come from.

Sunday dress, white ankle socks
folded over, edged in lace,
shiny shoes. In her fist,
she holds a yellow flower.

Birthed of innocence, her
essence steeped in wonder,
but this world isn't what she'd
hoped for or imagined.

How did she end up here,
lonely and confused, feeling

she doesn't belong? There
just isn't enough tenderness.

She tries pleasing the people
who want to mold her, but that
doesn't work. Finally, she recalls
what she used to know.

She needn't push so hard
or strain to make everyone happy.
She can connect to the lightness
and joy from that other place.

The seer says she's here to grow,
to show the world an original love.

The Hush

This is the calm I've been seeking,
softness of a quail's call,
mother bird tending
to her tiny offspring.
Wind rustling silver dollar
eucalyptus leaves to whisper
through my open window.
High above in the atmosphere,
the hum of a jet's engine.
Then a luscious silence.
Just now the *tee tee tee*
of a wren-tit, followed by
the dawn blessing of chickadees.

previously published in the San Luis Obispo Tribune, April 30, 2025

Robin is a mother, daughter, friend, writer, and photographer. She has spent her career working as a journalist or non-profit manager while writing essays and poems on the side. Her work has appeared in *Amaranth Journal, Snapdragon Journal, Amethyst Review, This I Believe* radio program, and in *Trailway News* magazine. She lives in N.E. Georgia with two hoodlum cats.

Infrasound

The cat on my lap sighs.
Subtle soft sound
Tiptoeing across the room,
Spreading comfort in small decibels.

That sigh joins its
Cousins of muted cacophony
That is a balm
In this sometimes afflicting world.

A baby's murmur as she settles into sleep.
The patter of rain when you have no plans.
The click of the front door's lock
when your grown children are under your roof
Like chicks beneath your wings.

People love a sizzling symphony.
Or thundering ocean roaring its beauty.
But for me, that sigh, these small, soft sounds
Are the remedy for the raw edges of my soul.

Sheila Lynch-Benttinen has been writing poetry her whole life, but recently started submitting poems in the last decade. She writes short haiku and long poems, some rhyming, some not. She was a 2024 Pushcart Prize nominee. She lives south of Boston with her husband, daughter, and border collie.

Surf The Noise

I left the digitally connected world

no longer tethered to the noise

I am divorced from the artificial light

out to wide-open beach in the late evening

a hush but not total silence

the soft rolling waves with soothing rhythm

though I know the ocean has many personalities

tonight, it is a napping water world with sparkles

the clear sky full of diamonds and the Milky Way necklace

gazing at the eternal,

I slowly quiet the voices in my head

I have learned to meditate into the stillness

become one with the One

recharged I see a plane and a distant satellite

and return to the modern world

with the ability to surf the noise

Lynn Without An E

my friend Lynn without an e
    taught me to look, really look
instead of just waiting for peonies in October
    I am trying to appreciate each season
lessons in how to silently look, really look
    now noticing the subtle beauty of a wide
November sky
    magnificent Orion hunting the winter solstice
crystal ice palaces of January
    deep hushed calm after a February blizzard
tiny shoots of green in March
    sprightly, happy daffodils along a roadside in April
along the magnificent path to the opulent bearded iris
    and then comes my radiant summer
I am taking lessons
    in appreciating the all of the all
silently wide open looking
    while having formerly taken for granted
the improbable gift of being alive

Church of Soft Snow in the Forest

tender fell the snow

        in the silent forest

except for whispering movements

        of the crimson cardinal wings

hushed cathedral of pines

        my soft padded footsteps barely

registered a sound

        as I view unique white snowflakes

dropping like slow angels

        and deep viridian green boughs

lightly iced with white powder

        I decided that the cardinals were literal

both birds and special assistants to the holy
in my silent winter church
as they led me through the
towering nave of pines
into the sanctuary's low sweet choir of chirps
my Irish kin believe cardinals
are visits from our ancestors
who am I to disagree?
the battered outside world
is far, far away as I pray
for our species
in the silence of the
Church of Soft Snow in the Forest

John Peter Beck was raised in a milltown on Lake Michigan in Michigan's Upper Peninsula. He is a recently retired professor in the labor education program at Michigan State University, where he still co-directs a program that focuses on labor history and the culture of the workplace, Our Daily Work/Our Daily Lives. His poetry has been published in a number of journals, including *The Seattle Review*, *Another Chicago Magazine*, *The Louisville Review*, and *Passages North*, among others.

The Sweet Movement

I agree.
We should expose
this nonsense,
the constant negotiation
of romance.

Your eyes affirm:
"Yes, it is not worth
the hassle." Yet,

I still think
about the gasp
for breath that follows
each kiss, the sweet
movement of air
when a woman
walks away.

The Geography of Absence

It is defined
by what is not

on the landscape,
a sneaking

suspicion that there
was something

just a moment ago.
Important things may

have happened here,
marked only by the faint outline

of loss, perhaps
a slight rise, a slight

depression in the earth.

The map of absence

has a key,

measured out

in the degrees of emptiness,

a sliding scale

which varies

for each of us.

Maren Chavez is a mother and scientist whose poetry occupies the liminal, exploring themes of inheritance, identity, and the intimate, transformative experiences of motherhood.

Dovetailed

The curve of my body fits
perfectly into
the gaps left by yours.
Dovetailed together like
notches in a log,
each groove carefully carved and
delicately assembled.
Building onto each other:
out and up and
always forward.
A new home and hearth,
sanctuary
in the wild of
the unknown.

8PM on a Tuesday

We lay side by side in your toddler-sized bed,
my knees crunched in because
even my body at 5'2 is too long.
Mama, can we cuddle?
you ask, and I think I could cry from
how wonderful that sounds,
coming from lips that came from me.

The dimple by my eye
that looks like a whisker
makes sense when I see it on you.
And it's not even because
I am seeing myself in you,
but because it's a feature of your own
that only appears when you smile.
A feature that I have learned to love on myself
because it belongs to you.

But of course,

I don't say any of this out loud.

Sure, I mumble as I snuggle into your chest.

Your breath on my hair,

I look up and

we both give a grin.

You close your eyes and

drape your tiny arm around me —

the outside of my body

meeting what came from within —

and I think I understand what it feels like to

be held by the entire universe.

Twin-Sized Heartache

God, she's so small —

I think as I tuck you into your brand-new bed.

Four years old:

vast sheets overwhelming your tiny body,

ocean blue, push and pull,

washing you ashore with

the tide.

I remember placing you in your crib,

three days old:

bed sheets like white space,

the most perfect poem swaddled within.

God, she's so small —

I thought as I stood over you,

watching to see what the story of you would

become.

All I could see, though,

was a piece of furniture engulfing my baby,

and the weight of responsibility engulfing me.

What have I done?

What do I do?

It didn't cross my mind that, eventually,

you would outgrow your crib,

that you would grow in

the most beautiful way.

I look at you now,

small body swathed in twin-sized heartache,

a grin like the sun.

I know that one day

you'll grow out of this bed, too,

but for now,

I will just lay with you.

Navila Nahid is a writer and published poet, currently residing in Brooklyn, NY. Her published works can be found in *Cream City Review, Chestnut Review, samfiftyfour, Pangyrus Lit*, and *The Dream Gods* anthology. She also has a social media presence on Instagram as @navilanahidpoetry

The Radical Act of

Waking up With the Sun

lacquered dark
resounds
a sometimes, moon

carving itself
palpable
upon witching hour

and I prone
watch—
a revolution

untame
a symphony
an agony

til dawn
and its unspun gold
devours skin

raw liminality
ravishing
holy

and I vigil
warm—
open-eyed

i don't mean to alarm anyone, but i've decided to be ridiculously optimistic and hopeful about life

about the next day

and the next

and each day

the sun

hits horizon

drowns bloody

there's joy

in the red and blue of waters

of bodies

the way

sinew curls the bones

bends the knee

for love

for grief

& i provoke

hemorrhage

of undeniable hope

& fall

with joy &

dance

dance

until i am safe

to roost

to root

this wound

that needs me

missing

Tekesia Haynes is the articulation of art in verse, prose, and script. A writer, poet, essayist, and educator from Antigua, she embodies the legacy of great authors who wrote worlds into being. Her work intertwines the sound of Shakespeare, Dostoyevsky, Lamming and Walcott, weaving classic influences into contemporary and Caribbean explorations of grief. *Grief's Morbid Monologues* is a silent rebellion, a eulogy giving voice to women's woes, often ostracized in the public psyche.

Depression and Denial

I am the creature that suckles
from the udder of the uncanny
latched to the uterus, an ulcer,
orbiting in ovaries
the tenant
paying monthly penance with presence.

I appear:
a herpetic abscess,
allured to absence,
a gnostic ghost grieving,
gaunt at the gallows,
inflicting grievous harm
to the ovum in orison of ovulation.

My posture, a gibbet,
detained to inevitably exit

as bloodcloths and liquid bane
on barren breeches.

My disposition; discharge.
To be, or not to be: that is the question
dueling my doctrine; a depressive dirge.
I stain as salutations.
invoking
enduring embarrassment as etiquette
I, bistre bracts of menstrual blood,
blossom a bill.

O, I die.
the potent poison quiet o'ercrows my spirit,
this skull, exiting her earth
will return,
the rest is silence. Dies.

Bargaining

Bare, I bled
in this barren bouquet of bluebells.
Dust, bale, by broom's dusk:
emptied, evoking an eclipse
in the mist of motive, mother,
her mien; wilt womb.

What is woman; without will
to warm this earth with a ward?
Woe to woman, deceased in womb,
doomed in bleak bosque.
Wrath originated in the ovaries as obituaries,
obtesting to gods.

I took by th' throat the circumcised dog and smote him thus,
at what end will this harrowed haint prove
thyself a saint?

Woman, my existence is fueled by fate;
I am black, and have not
these soft parts of conversation.

Warm worry with the wonder of life;
sever the sully of sterile security,
endure until your end,
concern not
of the finale that forms
as fertile failure
beneath the soul.

I beg,
bloom in this bituminous buoy.

E. D. Lloyd-Kimbrel [whose car masquerades as a branch library] is a New Jersey native residing in New England. Over the years and in-between various employments, academic endeavors, geographical locations, and life events, she has published biographical, critical, and scholarly essays along with assortments of poems and creative non-fiction. Her poetry chapbook Matrimonies [Finishing Line Press] was released in 2023.

Before The Pleiades Were Stars

Before the Pleiades were stars
they danced
unselfconsciously,
unconscious, unconscienced.
Before their home glided airless
they danced with wild abandon,
unknowing, unknown.
Before the pressure made them diamonds
their restless feet made oceans sparkle,
as spray whirled ’round them
when they had no admirers
and could run from joy alone.

Before the world was as it is

they had no thought of distance,

deliberate, apart.

Their hair was free,

their movements graceful,

directionless without confusion,

without forever watching,

rushing, unaware.

Later symmetry was found in night

beyond untamed seas,

which were before the Pleiades were stars

and we were the race of men.

previously published in Matrimonies [Finishing Line Press, 2023]: 2.

Anna Kuerner

after Wyeth

Sun streamed through
        the panes and withered hands
veins marked blue
        by the ice wash water
rubbed together
        to bring long-dead warmth
from weather
        forever to be frozen.
Dim eyesight
        stared out at snow
Glared fierce white
        by the incessant sun.
It had pained
        the eyes to look but when
the day waned
        the loneliness hurt more
so the hands
        again went into ice
and golden bands
        of light gave way to dark.

previously published in Permafrost (Winter 1987): 27.

Sandra Beth Levy [she/her] is a retired psychologist who passionately practiced the healing art of psychotherapy for over 40 years and is now pursuing her dream of immersing herself in creative writing and spoken-word performance. She raised two biracial poet sons while honoring her Jewish-feminist identities. Her social and personal histories weave their way through her writing as she explores intricacies of love, loss, aging, and awe of nature. She has won local poetry slams and published poems with Anomaly Poetry, Small Gems Press, Arcana Poetry Press, *A Curious Moon, The Vagabond's Verse, SHINE, The Poetry Lighthouse, Viridine Literary*, and a creative nonfiction piece with *The Orange Rose.* Find her on Instagram @slevy43.

Diamonds On Water

I came across a frog
who spoke to me through wide eyes
in frog language.
I shrugged my shoulders, laughed
and smiled, since I don't speak
frog tongue.
Bells rang nearby
from Trinity Episcopal church,
reminded me of Men's religions.
Women once acknowledged
religion sprouts from a womb
not from a rib that belonged to a man.
I came upon a pair of swans
preening peacefully in the bay.
I wondered what origin stories
frogs and swans share on their journeys;
if religion is in their vocabulary.
One swan glided gracefully
into a ray of shimmering water,

reflected afternoon sun,
became ensconced in magic light.
And there you were my college sweetheart,
deceased too soon from a cancer
that invaded your spine,
a walker whose legs shrunk
and failed to carry you
anymore.
Holding your hand
days before death
you told me,
whenever you see diamonds on water
I will be there.
And now I can decipher
religious speak of frogs and swans
on daily walks by the bay,
liturgy of image
eternal presence
blinding brilliance –

Salted Fingers

One morning sunshine wafts through your window
and heals what was once heavy
A feather gently grazes the crevasse of your elbow
rocks the love you've nursed since childhood
Despite quivering bones and eons of leaden despair
your soul surrenders
Tears drop like dew in a rainbow down your cheeks
salt your fingers with promise—
Become rain to grow the seed of you
planted deep in soothing soil
You are reborn as fledgling sprouts
rise like dough from replenished earth

David W. Berner is the author of more than a dozen works of fiction and memoir. He's been honored by the Chicago Writers Association, the Eric Hoffer Awards, the National Association of Independent Writers and Editors, and others. His short stories, essays, and poetry have been published in several publications, including the *Chicago Tribune, Southword* [the Munster Literature Centre in Ireland], *Write Launch, Beyond Words,* and

Mocking Owl Roost Literary Magazine. Berner has been honored as the Writer-in-Residence at the Jack Kerouac Project and at the Ernest Hemingway Birthplace Home and Museum.

Blue Morning

Look above the shadowed branches,
toward the reflective light,
that turns the heavens blue.
They say it's magic why the sky
is the color of melancholy,
the shade of sadness.
Look above it all to infinity,
beyond the mystery,
toward the vastness that awaits
the searching soul and the
grace of gifts arriving.

Caitlin Dunn is a finalist for The Poetry Lighthouse Award 2025. Her poems have appeared in *The High Shelf Literary Journal*, *Hip Pocket Press*, *The Journal of Short Fiction and Poetry*, *Cozy Ink Press*, *The Poetry Lighthouse*, and more. Caitlin currently lives in Denver, Colorado, with several pets and many books. You can find more of her work on Instagram @caitlindunnwrites.

Presage

Terrifyingly,
everything does get better.
My fingers stained bright

with raspberries, whipped
cream and honey, I drink dry
Cabernets and dance

like I used to: hands
overhead, blind to the world.
Still—out the window,

I notice the cold
weather changing its shape like
a yet-healing bruise.

Linda M. Crate [she/her] is a Pennsylvanian writer whose poetry, short stories, articles, and reviews have been published in a myriad of magazines, both online and in print. She has fifteen published chapbooks, the latest being: *not your piñata* (Alien Buddha Publishing, June 2025).

the quiet of the forest

soothes my soul,
the trees give me compassion
and kindness;

the wind whispers to me
secrets of old and new and blows
away every worry—

the creek washes away all
my pain and anger,

sometimes the silence is broken
by the song of crows or the
chittering of chipmunks;

but is always magical to simply be
in the forest—

watch as the sun falls through the
trees and glitter in such soft
psalms,

i am often alone when i am there
but i don't mind;

i have always found beauty in
places others don't think to look,
and there is such magic in the forest—
she always calls me back, for she
accepts me wild and all, never
wishing to tame me or cage me, simply
heal me in ways my fellow humans cannot.

Sharon E. Ludan holds a B.A. from the College of New Jersey and an M.S. from Boston University. As an American diplomat, Ludan has lived and worked in many countries throughout the world. Her work has been published by Proverse Hong Kong, Wingless Dreamer, Quillkeepers Press, Unleash Press; the Kansai Scene; the *OSIPP Journal*, and elsewhere. Sharon hopes you enjoy these poems!

And Now for Some Nice News

I'm tired of the dark side
he said,

and I envied his vow
to write only of the good,

joy and beauty
and the saving graces

[saving us from ourselves
and all the scary depths
of the dark side.]

I could do that if I tried.

Why, just this morning
at the supermarket,

the tattooed cashier with
the close-cropped hair

spoke gently

to her customer
fumbling at the pin pad;

while we
in the queued audience
looked away patiently.

Her kindness
hung in the air,
softly diffusing around us,

and it clung to me
when I left.

previously published in Thriving, Exsolutas Press, 2024

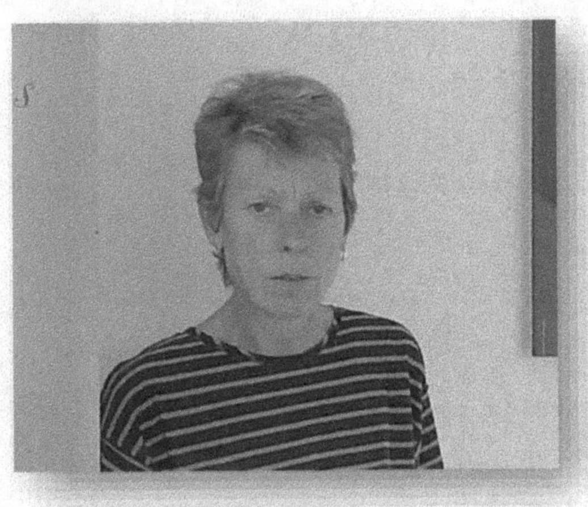

Sally Mills graduated as an artist and went on to pursue a career devoted to nature conservation. She has written/illustrated three publications: her debut memoir, *Island to Island*, and accompanying Photograph Collection, together with the production of illustrations for a children's book, Boomy the Bittern. With a drive and motivation to inspire people about nature and our role within it, she has become captivated by the world of poetry. She has had children's poems published by the Dirigible Balloon and has recently had poems selected by *The Toy and Little Thoughts Press* magazines. Her poetry for adults is due to appear in five anthologies.

The Samaritan

From the time you answer it is agreed,
silence has so much more to say than words,
its listening, not a sign to proceed
with verbal verbatim you think you've heard.
Your composed breath on the line is enough,
inviting me to pause, sit back and breathe,
as you can understand, life's been rough,
and patience today will help to relieve
the pent-up stress from the recent down days.
Your kindness, my cue to make the first move,
I speak in riddles, I'm stuck in the maze
of life, and unsure when it will improve.
Our pact is broken, but still dignified,
reflecting, 'just give it time'—your reply.

Hugh Findlay's writing and photography have been published worldwide. In addition to many awards, his nominations include: a Pushcart Prize for poetry 2020, Best of the Net for poetry 2025, Best Microfiction 2024, and Best of the Net for photography 2024. IG: @hughmanfindlay. Web: https://www.hughmanfindlay.com

Well, So What?

For the feel of it

I sat naked in the rain.

But the judge said

I couldn't do it in public.

And I said

I couldn't in the house either.

So in jail

the roof felt the rain instead.

And all night

the roof giggled.

previously published in Barzakh magazine, Spring 2020.

Angelina Oberdan Brooks is a writer and professor. The poems in her chapbook, *Heavy Bloom*, were largely generated when she camped across the country with her three dogs. Since those living-out-of-her-car summers, she has fallen in love, embraced step-motherhood, and spent a lot of time healing. As Johanna Hedva writes, “The most anti-capitalist protest is to care,” and in that way, her life and her poems have become a series of tiny, daily protests—against production determining our worth, against busyness becoming a way of life, against obfuscating physical pain. She recently completed a writing residency at the Weymouth Center. Her poems have been published or are forthcoming in various journals, including *Halcyone, Split Rock Review, Litmosphere,* and *Cold Mountain Review.*

Orchid

in all-day sunlight

on the kitchen windowsill

the orchid eats air

pink fleshy petals

& roots that wend their way out

topside graceful they

reach for the mist of

dinners spray of dishes

& other muggy

mercies this orchid

is an accountant of dew

& light—how it sifts

through canopy &

kapok or horizontal
blinds easy as a

tattered yard cat this
orchid throws open six blooms
in winter's low light

& Scorpio moon
she thrives here witness
to the tenor of

our murmuring day—
to-day the way my hands are
always reaching for you.

David Radavich has published a variety of poetry, drama, essays, and reviews. His plays have been performed across the U.S. and in Europe. His latest books are *UNTER DER SONNE / UNDER THE SUN: German Poems* (Deutscher Lyrik, 2021) and *HERE'S PLENTY* (Cervena Barva, 2023).

Cancer Photo

I am bald now,
neither man nor woman,
in winter wrapped
in fur
up to the neck
against a naked
tree that
stands as a wall
in the flashing night.
A scarf drapes
the neck like a noose.
All history stops
at the frame
defining
the bare self.

Who knows

where the smile

goes—

back to

childhood?—

or what cells

eat their way home

unseen

unheard

in the black air.

Evan Thomas Cummings is a New York City based poet who was nominated by Brooklyn Poets for their 2024 Poem of the Year award for his poem, “Everything at all Times.” Previous poems of his have been published by *Ink Magazine*, *VoyageLA*, & others. His work deals primarily in themes of grief, transience, & the theologies of addiction/recovery— he’s glad to be alive & kickin’.

In Place of Gratitude

The cats have beef & liver feast
with giblets in some gravy
while I watch The Last Waltz,
eat pad Thai, & try not to be sad.

There is plenty to be thankful for;
I just became an uncle,
& my sister says he sleeps well on the
sheepskin that I bought.

My mother's boyfriend has the same name
as my father, who is
dead; Tom takes her down to
Boston for her biweekly transfusion.

I haven't lived in Deerfield Massachusetts
for six months,
& I do not drive a RAV-4
with a fucked-up alternator.

No, it's not a winter coat:
mom's leather jacket from the eighties,

but it makes me feel Freewheelin'
through the breeze & ginkgo-stink.

This is a city for the very rich &,
often, very poor; Joan said
it's also for the very young,
but I think she meant, 'sad.'

I'm thirty now, I'm single, &
the manuscript's not finished—
all other ways of saying,
it's been five years since I drank.

In place of gratitude,
acceptance; you see, things are as they've been,

& Joe the meth-head says
all liquor tastes like guilt from here on out.

I have a couple goals, I guess I'd say;
sure, maybe one or two, but
if it's all the same,
I'd want the name that feels right in my mouth.

I'd want to read all of the poems
that were written by sad people,
& teach curriculums about
more liberty & shelter.

One of my 7th graders asked me
to print Mary's Wild Geese
so she could hang it in her bedroom.
I am doing a good job.

There is nothing else to do,
nothing but to come & go
with the bullets of to-do list
I tear out to end the day:

"pay your bills, write a poem,
say, 'I love you,' & don't drink."
If anything, I guess I'm saying
it's all maddeningly simple.

Brittany Morgan is a poet and writer who earned her BA in English with a concentration in Creative Writing from Longwood University in 2020, and her MFA in Creative Writing from West Virginia Wesleyan College in 2023. She is also a Poetry Editor for *Heartwood Literary Magazine* and is currently working on several writing projects.

Praise to the Darkened Bedroom

If I'm thinking about the darkest place
I've ever been, I'd go
back to my old childhood bedroom
at five years old—back to that
night I first felt the presence of
something real, something other
than myself. That night, I opened the
creaking, wooden door,
climbing into my bed with toy teddies
and tiny guardrails in place.
But I couldn't sleep a single second
at all that night. I stayed
alert, constantly and silently repeating
'Jesus loves me, this I know'—a chant,
a prayer, a spell—saving me from
all my sleep-deprived darkened fears.
And in that fearful stillness,
in that space filled with waiting
I found myself—my true, quiet, soul—
self—for the first time.

And I felt at home.

Cassie Andresen (she/they) is a queer poet and musician based in Seattle. She writes and performs art exploring feminism, queerness, sobriety, grief, and disability advocacy. You can read their poem "Silvers" in *Testament: A Rural Anthology* from Backwoods Literary Press, and their poem "I Can't See the Ending" in *PROGRESS (not perfection)* from 40 West Arts. Her work is inspired by her experiences as a dyke in love while navigating surrounding illness and death. She can often be found creating music with her wife, crafting new non-alcoholic beverages, and finding a body of water to jump in.

The Crash

One day

after years of being terrified of this precise

feeling

I came to the realization that I truly cherished

the sensation of my feet being cold

Before piecing together that healing might derive

from both space and thorough, loving energy

This experience occurred in my new home

icy water crashing over my feet

and instead of clenching my body and soul

I fucking sighed

A relief and a loosening

The liberation of a long-lived ache

The next time I attempted to recreate

this moment with myself

I slipped, fell, and cut my hand
As I gazed down
at the sea grime on my ass
while perched on a rock in a park
in my wet underwear
Ripped shorts in hand
Blood dripping down my fingers
I thought how honest this living metaphor felt

How sometimes being alive this openly
sets you up to crash
and that this fall might have just spread me
bare enough
for the next bright moment to come.

Cody Draco is a queer poet, settled but never stagnant, creatively restless in the ever-shifting United States landscape. His poem, "Anatomy of the Human Experience", was selected as the winner of the 2025 Chaffin/Kash Prize presented by the Kentucky State Poetry Society. His collection, *Spirit of the Cowboy*, received the Voyages of Verses Book Award from OneTribune. Unflinching yet deeply human, his poetry pushes boundaries in an intentional effort to code a new masculinity. His work has appeared in *Santa Clara Review* and elsewhere.

Exit Interview with the Elusive 'I'

but what if you are only ever
brutal balm for the salvaged soul
cycled through those bodies no longer burning
in history's insatiable furnace
who believed the future would always
be fueled by the coal they mined
because life goes on and it arrives on time?

I suppose I would reside
reclined with my feet up relaxed in role
healing the hurt before they hurled rocks
at the glass house where my heartbreak lived
voyeuristically seen in a mid-scream
that long went unheard
only for a vow of silence earned
to slice through this savage beastly world
with the precision of Masamune's master sword

F. E. Smith is a Michigan-born university student by day, and a writer, poet, and playwright by night.

moonlight rapture

sea and sky dissolve
shoreline horizon
like a pill on the tongue
of the sickle-sharp moon
with soft and hollow stars
made of molten light
liquid fire seeping
into the deep black and
nighttime blue

prickling stones tickle
bare feet and meet
soft sands
and sink down
around ankles
sifting between toes
cooling soothing sinking

sinking

into the maw of the

headlight-bright moon

like the night sky

is a highway

and i am a doe

fat from fawn season

stuck staring at the oncoming

angel sent from metal gods

like it has something

for me other than

the other side

Laura Ribitzky's poems have appeared in *Zone 3*, the *San Diego Poetry Annual*, and the *Poets Underground* Anthology. She holds an MA in Conflict Resolution from the University of Massachusetts Boston and a JD from the City University of New York School of Law. She is currently pursuing an MFA from San Diego State University, where she was a recipient of the Sarah B. Marsh-Rebello Scholarship for Poetry.

Packing List for Emigrants

I only take what I need:
books, clothes, essential documents
[always with translations] — but mostly

books in my mother tongue
that I soon won't know how
to read anymore. New words

crowd the old ones out
before I have time
to tell them goodbye.

Alex Dawson is a writer, mom, wildlife photographer, and ESL teacher from Toronto. She recently published a nature fact poetry anthology, entitled *Upon Learning That*, which reached #1 in poetry anthologies on Amazon. She published her photo-poetry book, *All these Living Things*, in the summer of 2024. Alex has also been published by *The Queen's Quarterly*, *The Bombay Literary Review*, *Turning Leaf Journal*, Livina Press, and Gather Poets. She writes with constant curiosity and a desire to examine the threads of connection between nature, culture, and identity. Alex can be found on Instagram and Substack @alexdawcreates.

Confessional

I don't wear my heart on my sleeve,
I wear it in my eyes. I eat my heart

like an apple when this world offers
no other sweetness. I hold my heart

out to everything. It thrums like
a red hummingbird in July. I have

never been anything but radically
tender. I can't help it, there's just

so much still left to love.

Jessica Noè-Mougis (she/her) is a poet and dancer whose work explores the intersections of spirituality, motherhood, artistry, and personal transformation. Her poems have sprouted into songs and choreography, which are currently being developed into a full-length musical project called *True North*. In 2024, she released her first poetry collection, *She Holds the World*. Jessica has also been published in Half and One. She lives in

Ridgewood, New Jersey, with her husband and three small children, who color her world. Her writing can be found on Instagram @jessica.noe.mougis_writer

What Remains

What is it that we are, anyway?

Nonno, you became a child again
speaking Piemontese and Latin
innocent, naive and charming

today I visited your brother
not who he was
his stubbornness still here
the mind that defined him
has left already

so who is it that remains?
and where did the other go?
who is this version that breaks our hearts?

just when I think
i've got a grasp
it all blows away

What is it that we are, anyway?

Shannon Vistins was born and raised in southeastern Ohio. She is a teacher who now lives in the San Fernando Valley of California with her husband and two children. She is a member of the Soldner Center Poetry Collaborative.

Sunscald

Plant leaves roll
and cup themselves
from harm.
Only the wish
to languish
remains.
[The tomb-like cool
of a downstairs bedroom.]
Somewhere,
a desert looming,
creates the urge to
bolt:
that is, to abruptly
flower,
before the time
of blooming.

Andrea Tillmanns lives in Germany and works full-time as a university lecturer. She has been writing poetry, short stories, and novels in various genres for many years. Her poems and stories have been published in *The Prairie Schooner, The Adirondack Review, Clarion,* and other journals and anthologies. More information about the author and her texts can be found on her website www.andreatillmanns.de.

Beginning of Spring

At the foot of the ivy-covered wall,
the animal glistens in the sun,
its black-brown scales shimmering.
Lizard spots dart through the sunbeams
amidst the evergreen foliage
and pause once more:
The promise of warmth
is already in the air.

Kyle [she/her] is a queer and neurodivergent writer healing her relationship with language and words after being a lifelong engineer. She is inspired by the resonance found between each other and the world around us. She is a Jersey Girl at heart but calls the Midwest home in Madison, Wisconsin, immersed in a world of music, climbing, and community.

Kintsugi

for Annie & Gen

Every afternoon I take my dog on a walk and we pass the woman who lives on the corner – and one must pause in the gallery of golden afternoon sun filling gaps of foliage and blooms – the creation of an artist whose weathered and loving hands work tender and knowing for her garden in a way it cannot ask for – quietly understood in the creases carved by time and memory now nourished by the earth from sowing dreams and roots into the fresh soil – nurturing growth by pruning only what is necessary or finding a thread in the kitchen drawer to support two stems against one another as they reach in the same direction – guiding the new leaves and buds as they unfurl their petals into open palms cupped to capture and cherish the light and warmth of a life they imagine – cradled and radiating a love within to grow a home – perhaps for a tiny bee in need of a place to rest on a cool autumn night – or just a passerby in search of the words for what hasn't been made for them but is beautiful all the same.

Kate Champagne lives in the Twin Cities. A lover of languages, she holds a Master's in Spanish from Middlebury Language Schools in Vermont with a specialization in linguistics. She teaches Spanish by day and writes in the in-between, especially moved to give voice to the poetry of the everyday experience and the complexities of the interior life. Kate has been published in *Allegro Magazine* and has work forthcoming in Chariot Press and *Veritas Journal*.

Late October Night

A maple raises
bare arms
to the sliver
of vermilion
low in the sky

it understands
surrendering
all but the
skeleton
of itself

it understands
the grief
and relief
of waning

Emma is a mother and English teacher. She has published poetry in various literary journals and magazines. She writes flash fiction, short stories, and novels. She is currently writing her sixth novel.

Fall

If I allow myself,
I will fall.

Amidst gnarly thorns,
snags and deep lashes,
I shall find you,
buried deep in undergrowth,
waiting to be reborn.

Sheer, lucid need
stretches sinews taut,
reaching for an invisible you:
a mirage on the horizon,
disappearing in plain sight.

To fall is to erase myself
yet how sweet the destruction—

marrying heaven and hell
in one heady gulp,
unwrapping barbed wire layers
until I rediscover you,
fall into your chest:
smudging, blurring identities.

If I fell into a mirror,
would you catch me?
Be my breathing hole?

I sense your presence
beneath reflections,
luring as a troubled ghost,
unable to settle —without me.

Tim Boardman is a poet based in West Yorkshire whose work explores the quiet beauty of everyday life, the shifting landscapes of the North, and the complexities of human connection. Drawing inspiration from nature, memory, and his local heritage, his poems are both grounded and lyrical, often balancing emotional honesty with wry observation. His writing has been featured in local readings, community arts projects, and online literary platforms. Tim's commitment to accessible, resonant poetry has made him a distinctive voice within the regional arts scene.

Hotel Breakfast

On holidays
I hide Coco Pops
beneath my muesli—
like some child
hiding the truth—
and girls in pyjamas—
in the breakfast restaurant
(the same girls I saw
outside McDonald's,
crying at 10pm—
fight over dried-out eggs,
fried and scrambled.)
A framed lettering proclaims
HAP
PIN
ESS.
It smells of waste.
A slot machine glows.
'I need to

gather the troops.'

Flip-flops and Crocs

are the footwear.

No one has slept.

Coffee drips from the machine,

spilling into the carpet,

its pattern long erased.

An older man,

belly over belt,

trails a young waiter.

And in the corner—

the slot machine

still glowing.

I've got a taste in my mouth

of the hotel

like something has been living

in there overnight

Roberta Batorsky is a poet, science journalist, and college educator. She is in several online and in-person poetry and fiction critique groups and has a poetry book called Perihelion, published last month by Prolific Pulse Press. She is published in *Fine-Lines, Delaware Valley Poets, Poets for Science, Prolific Pulse Press poetry compilations (Social Possibilities and Unhoused), NJ Bards, NewVerseNews,* and *Heron Clan.* She has also been a freelance editor/reviewer of *Life Sciences* textbooks. She co-edits the *Heron Clan* poetry publication. She teaches in a New Jersey state prison. Her science blog is at https://solipsistssoiree.blogspot.com. She writes on topics as varied as her interests and currently teaches Biology at a New Jersey youth corrections facility. @RobertaBatorsky_poetry [Instagram]

Birds of the Forest Floor

Drill beneath the canopy to see
carrion-eaters clear the understory.
Thankless job for
hawks, vultures, ravens, crows:
never unemployed!

The ungainly clean-head hoppers'
small-eyed, blinkless stares pierce
rend unearth scrounge the darkness
debride wounds of the dying, dead.

Hesitate to judge the forest owlet's
borrowed nest of carcasses' decaying flesh:
Cleansers take abandoned nests.

Nourish they who nourish you,
that nourish the forest

to make it capable and fertile
if may be done.
if may be born,
if life could reinvent
and not ruin
as has done me.

For the buzzard, quick of eye,
find in its stare, kindness of a mother,
even sacrifice.
Sharp beaks and talons gripping
and me,
hard-gripping back in the unslept night.

What no one wants to see—
the recyclers make-fit:
the silky, lush-needled undersoil.

About Us

Quillkeepers Press, LLC is a small indie press and indie author resource group. We publish themed anthologies on a variety of topics, as well as provide resources and services to indie authors. We pride ourselves on the quality of our traditionally published titles, as well as our reasonably priced services for indie authors who prefer to do it themselves. It is a deep passion of ours to help as many writers' voices as possible be heard. As indie artists ourselves, we understand most creatives operate within a strict budget. Therefore, it has always been a priority of ours to keep our rates reasonable. Our corporate climate is not one of profit but one of helping bring dreams to fruition. Our motto sums it up best: *"Reading between the lines, to make your words take flight"*.

We produce between 3 and 6 anthologies annually. We don't charge artists to be published in our anthologies, although tips are welcome through Submittable.com to cover the cost of the ad space, ISBN number registration, copyright fees, as well as other overhead costs.

As writers ourselves, we understand how challenging the market can be and how difficult it is to get work into the hands of a larger audience. Therefore, we accept and encourage our contributors to submit both new and previously published compositions (as long as the previous publisher allows it). Too often, we find publishers who want exclusive rights to the work being published. This is counterproductive if the artist wants their message to reach as many people as possible. Having been in and studied the industry for years, our founder has concluded that many writers take great pride in their work and produce it for their own healing.

Furthermore, they share said work, hoping it helps others heal. For all the aforementioned reasons, it is our current policy to request non-exclusive rights to our contributors' work rather than exclusive rights. In essence, our artists are allowing us to borrow their prized writing, and we are incredibly grateful.

It is also for those same reasons that we consider ourselves an indie publishing services company, rather than a traditional publisher. Traditional publishing typically involves a lengthy contract, exclusive rights to work, and royalties. We would rather help wrap artists' products into a beautiful package and allow them to set their own parameters, price points, and keep all their royalties from sales.

On a final note, whether you have employed our services or lent us your voice in an anthology, thank you for entrusting us with your craft. If you would like to participate in a forthcoming anthology, please check out our Submittable page at www.submittable.com. For more information on our services, please visit our website www.quillkeeperspress.com

Keep the quill moving,

Stephanie Lamb, Founder, EIC

Quillkeepers Press, LLC

Other Books Produced by Quillkeepers Press

Soon, A New Day

A rise of the Phoenix-themed anthology of essays, memoirs, short stories, and poetry by various artist

Turning Dark into Light and Other Magic

Tricks of the Mind

A mental health-themed anthology of essays, memoirs, short stories, and poetry by various artists

Rearing in the Rearview

A parenting-themed anthology of essays, memoirs, short stories, and poetry by various artists

Verbal Vomit and Other Poetry and Prose

A poetry and prose collection by Stephanie Lamb

Tan Lines

A Summer Solstice-inspired anthology of memoirs, short stories, and poetry by various artists.

Bare Bones

A Halloween-inspired anthology of essays, memoirs, short stories, and poetry by various artists.

Snowdrifts

A Winter Solstice-inspired anthology of essays, memoirs, short stories, and poetry by various artists.

Sapling

A Spring equinox-inspired anthology of essays, memoirs, short stories, and poetry by various artists.

Dislocated

The debut poetry collection by Dylan Webster.

Botany of Gaia

A nature-inspired anthology of essays, memoirs, short stories, and poetry by various artists.

Harvest

A Fall equinox-inspired anthology of essays, memoirs, short stories, and poetry by various artists.

The Matador's Wife

A chapbook-length collection of poetry by Andrés Colón.

scars & lyres

A chapbook-length collection of poetry by ww harris.

Inspired

An art-inspired-by-art anthology of essays, memoirs, short stories, poetry, and artwork.

Smitten

A love-inspired anthology of essays, memoirs, short stories, and poetry.

High Water

A chapbook-length collection of poetry by Carrie Carter.

Notable Moons

A Chapbook-length collection of poetry by David Gunton.

My West

A chapbook-length collection of poetry by Jenifer Fox.

Lightwaves

A YA Historical Fiction novella

AmerAsian

A poetry collection by Kimberly McAfee.

The Savior and the Shadow Queen

A poetry collection by Kimberly McAfee.

Turning the Corner

A poetry collection by Lori Ulrich.

Purge & Bloom

A chapbook-length poetry collection by Brooks Decker.

Arranging Words

A chapbook-length poetry collection by Fran Abrams.

Words for Women

A chapbook-length poetry collection by Lori Heninger.

Lent Words

A chapbook-length poetry collection by Christine Moore.

Talking to Ghosts

A chapbook-length poetry collection by Jon Tobias.

A House with Bad Bones

A poetry collection by Adeline Tatum

The Wake of the Hound Dogs

A witty must-read novel by AD Matson

Alchemies, Arrivals

An eco-poetry chapbook collection by Sophia Pinto Thomas

Ikusei: Nurture

A carefully curated anthology of haikus by various authors.

Weaving the Light

A women's appreciation anthology from voices across the globe.

Interbeing

A chapbook-length poetry collection by Soraya Bakhbakhi

The House as Witness

A chapbook-length poetry collection by Veronica Tucker

First Draft of a Man

A Chapbook-length poetry collection by Connor Lynch

The Echoes We Make

A men's appreciation anthology from voices across the globe.

www.ingramcontent.com/pod-product-compliance
Lightning Source LLC
Chambersburg PA
CBHW011923050726
47591CB00009B/2315

* 9 7 8 1 9 6 9 6 0 1 0 6 4 *